PAiNT!

LANDSCAPES

A RotoVision Book, Published and Distributed by RotoVision SA, Rue Du Bugnon 7, 1299 Crans-Près-Céligny, Switzerland.

RotoVision SA, Sales & Production Office, Sheridan House, 112/116A Western Road, HOVE BN3 1DD, England. Tel: +44 (0) 1273 72 72 68 Fax: +44 (0) 1273 72 72 69. e-mail sales@RotoVision.com

Distributed to the trade in the United States: Watson-Guptill Publications, 1515 Broadway, New York, NY 10036. Copyright © RotoVision SA 1999. All rights reserved. No part of this publication may
10 9 8 7 6 5 4 3 2 1

Book design by Brenda Dermody, Dublin. Production and separations in Singapore by ProVision Pte. Ltd. Tel: +65 334 7720 Fax: +65 334 7721

PAiNT!

LANDSCAPES

BETSY HOSEGOOD

RotoVision

contents

Introduction

This book is a celebration of the landscape seen through the eyes of a selection of different artists. It seeks to show that there is no right or wrong way of painting a scene and that there is no perfect medium. The artists come in all guises and from many different countries and backgrounds. Some have impressive formal training, others are self-taught; some went to top art schools and colleges, others studied under individual artists. But what they all share is a love of the landscape and a talent for recreating it in paint.

When approaching the subject the artist can either decide to render its physical appearance as faithfully as possible or to capture its essence by portraying either the emotions it evokes or the power that surges under rock and tree. Most artists will say that they do a bit of both, but some render emotions more subtly than others. For example, while one artist may gently heighten colour for emotional impact, another might change colours and forms so much that the original scene is barely recognizable to the untrained eye.

One thing you will notice when scanning through this book is that although the paintings are loosely divided by medium, the styles within each group are often quite different. This is because the artists don't try to adapt their styles to suit the medium, as a beginner might do, but instead force the medium to conform to their will.

How the book works

Unlike other books on the market this one doesn't give an individual's opinion about a series of paintings. Instead the artists speak for themselves, explaining what motivated them to paint a particular image and the process by which they achieved it. Along the way we find out more about what makes an artist.

There are no difficult terms to understand or complex procedures to follow so even if you have never read a book on art before you will be able to enjoy this one. Information about particular techniques and other related items is separated from the main text so you can refer to it if you choose, and, on the basis that images say more than words, diagrams are used to exemplify how the artists composed their paintings.

One or more paintings is selected from the work of each artist to be examined in some detail. This is broken down into four categories so you can instantly refer to the sections which interest you. The first pages look at the artist's motivation and provide background information about the work. What first attracted the artist to the scene and how he or she responded

to it. Then you'll find an explanation of the artist's composition followed by his or her use of colour and finally any particular techniques used.

Composition

The second topic covered for each artist is composition. This is quite a technical subject and perhaps surprisingly can involve some complex mathematics. Luckily you don't need to know about it in detail to appreciate art, but if you want to become an artist yourself, it would definitely be worth taking a course on the subject or reading a specialist book. This book highlights just a few aspects of composition for each artist, giving a taste of what is possible.

Where landscapes are concerned probably the two most relevant compositional devices are the Golden Section (also called the Golden Mean) and the rule of thirds. The Golden Section was formulated by Vitruvius in the first century BC. He said that the harmonious relationship of unequal parts of a whole was achieved if the smaller was in the same proportion to the larger as the larger was to the whole. In mathematical terms this creates the sequence 1, 2, 3, 5, 8, 13, 21, 34 and so on which interestingly is a sequence often found in Nature – the way a shell increases in size or a tree forms a series of branches and twigs.

On canvas these proportions are created using a compass and ruler to divide the support into four unequal parts with one vertical and one horizontal line (see diagrams). Artists can either place the key focus where the lines intersect or arrange several subjects so that they fit into the different sections. They might place the horizon along the horizontal line, for example, so that the land area falls into the lower sections and place a large tree or the edge of a building so it fills one of the top sections or is dissected by the vertical line.

The Golden Section is complicated, so most artists today tend to use the more straightforward rule of thirds instead which is based along similar lines. Basically if you divide the support into thirds both vertically and horizontally, then the points where the vertical and horizontal lines intersect are considered the most pleasing positions for a focal point (see diagram below). Most landscape artists also like to place the horizon line along or close to one of the horizontal thirds because this tends to create pleasing proportions. Many artists do this subconsciously.

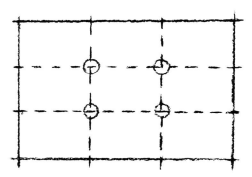

Rule of thirds

The Golden Section

The Golden Section refers to a precise division of the support along mathematical lines to create what can be considered the perfect proportions. To create a support divided along these lines refer to the diagrams right. Draw the measurements on paper first and then you can transfer them to several supports.

First decide on the width of the picture area and draw a horizontal line on paper this long from A to B (you can work to scale).

Draw a vertical line from B to C which is half the length of AB. Join C to A with a straight line. Now take a compass and put the point at C with the pencil end at B and draw an arc that intersects the line CA. Label this point D.

Now put the compass point at A with the pencil end at D and draw an arc that cuts through AB at E to a point directly below A at F. EB is in the same proportion to AE as AE is to AB.

Insert the compass point at E with the pencil at B and draw an arc to a point directly below E at G. Complete a rectangle as shown. Transfer the rectangle to your support complete with the horizontal and vertical lines and use them to plot your composition along the lines of the Golden Section.

Rule of thirds

The rule of thirds suggests that if you mentally divide the support into thirds the most pleasing positions for focal points are where the dividing lines intersect. Artists often place the horizon in a landscape painting along one of the thirds.

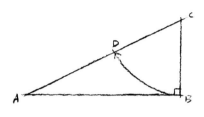

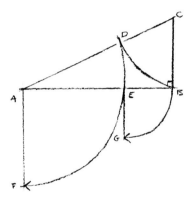

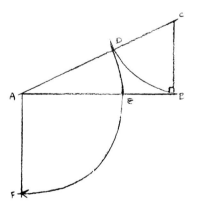

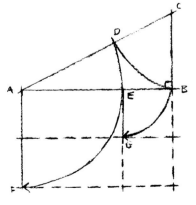

Colour

The fabulous colours of a beautiful painting are often taken for granted by the uninitiated, but amateur artists marvel at them because it takes so much practice and experience to mix the colours desired. The only way you can really appreciate the complexity of colour mixing is to try it for yourself, and as an artist the only way you can truly learn is through practice. Having said that, an understanding of the colour wheel and how colour works plus an insight into how paints are made will be of considerable help.

If you are just starting out as an artist or even if you consider yourself an experienced amateur, one of the easiest ways to learn about colour is to limit the ones you use. Start with a range of six to ten paints and try not to add to them until you have got to grips with the ones you have already. (See facing page for a good basic palette.)

The other important thing to do is buy quality colours and stick with them. Student quality paints are fine if you only intend to dabble or sketch, but they aren't usually as good as artists' quality paints and with watercolour in particular you may find your work starts to fade rapidly if you choose inferior materials. Also, if you start with student paints and then switch to artists ones you may find that the colours and strengths are different so you have to relearn how to use them. Paints even vary from brand to brand, so once you have found a type and make of paint that you like, continue with it.

Colour mixing

A colour wheel showing primary red, yellow and blue with secondaries orange, green and violet in-between is a very useful visual aid to getting to grips with the basics of colour mixing, but it is only a starting point. It can only show what happens when you mix adjacent colours, and so it cannot hope to show all there is to know. For example, some of the most useful artists colours are neutrals which are created by mixing opposite colours on the wheel. Adding just a little of the opposite colour is also a good way to mute a colour slightly.

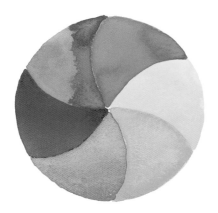

The other problem with the colour wheel is that in reality there are no single tubes of primary red, yellow or blue paint. So if an artist doesn't have primary yellow or red, how can he mix a true orange? The answer is that he can't really, but this doesn't matter. A huge range of wonderful oranges can be mixed by using a yellow which is either on the warm or cool side of primary yellow and a red which is also either warm or cool. Any colour which can't be readily mixed from a basic range in this way can be purchased separately – many artists add a green to their palette, such as viridian or another strong colour such as manganese violet, for example.

A good basic palette for a landscape artist might include two yellows, two reds and two blues, one warm and one cool version of each. The most popular and reliable are cadmium lemon (cool); cadmium yellow (warm); quinacridone violet or alizarin crimson (cool); cadmium red (warm); cerulean blue (cool); and French ultramarine (warm). It might also include two greens – viridian and chromium oxide green are good – although many artists prefer to mix their own greens from blues and yellows. In addition, no artist's palette is likely to be without a few earth colours – yellow ochre is popular, plus raw umber and burnt sienna, for example. A good white, such as flake white for oils or titanium white for other mediums is essential, except for watercolour, which many artists prefer to use pure, without the addition of white.

cadmium lemon   cadmium yellow   yellow ochre

alizarin   cadmium red   French ultramarine   cerulean blue

viridian   chromium oxide green   burnt sienna   raw umber

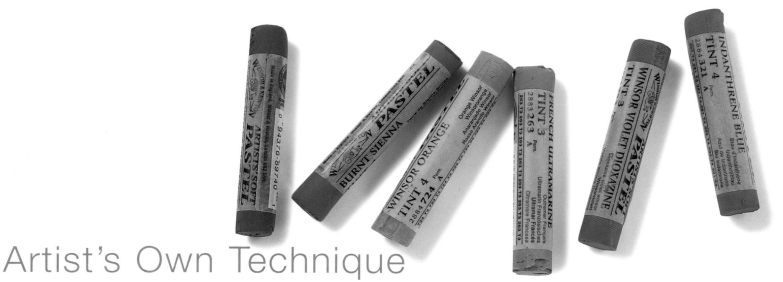

Artist's Own Technique

An artist's technique is a very personal thing, so even if two artists have been taught by the same person and use the same mediums, their styles are likely to be very different. This is, of course, part of the attraction of art. Artists can use their skills as a means of expression and interpret what they have learnt in different ways. Thus, although artists can learn a lot from each other, they can really only learn by experience and should never try to be exactly like one of their fellows. Because art is all about self-expression, this books shows some of the techniques used by the artists as seen through their own eyes. Sometimes this may seem a bit confusing because, for example, one artist may claim to create a lot of texture in a painting and yet that painting may have less textural interest than a painting by another artist who claims he has added hardly any texture. Remember that it is all relative and each artist is starting from a different position with different aims in mind.

Watercolour techniques

This is a wonderful medium for capturing landscape and even artists who prefer other mediums often start out with a watercolour sketch made on site. It is particularly good at capturing light, both in the sky and reflected from water and the landscape. True watercolour is worked without the addition of white paint, but a little Chinese white used to add sparkle is considered acceptable even by most purists. When a lot of white is used or even added to the paint by the manufacturer to create a more opaque paint, it is called gouache.

People who don't know much about watercolour sometimes associate it solely with the pale, moody paintings of Victorian ladies of leisure. This book shows that in the right hands it can be a dramatic and colourful medium which can be manipulated in all sorts of ways to create exciting effects.

Oil techniques

Artists who paint along traditional lines often opt for oils as their medium because of its impressive historical credentials. Art schools, past and present, helped to develop a code of practice for working in oils which artists can choose to adopt or ignore. However, some rules are ignored at the artist's peril because they have firm founding in scientific fact. One such rule is that of working 'fat over lean', i.e. with thick, oil-rich

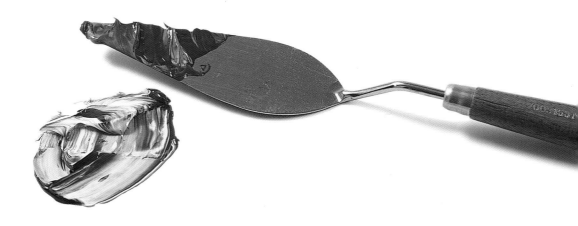

paint over thinner paint diluted with turpentine. This rule makes sense not only because the thinner base layers of paint dry quicker than thick paint, making it possible to progress faster yet still add textural interest at the end, but also because if you apply thinned paint over thick, oily paint, the finished paint layers may crack as they dry.

Acrylic techniques

This is a medium which was once scorned by collectors and purists, but is now gaining ground, mainly because artists are turning to it more and more. It has many advantages, not least that it can be used in the same way and to similar effect as watercolour or oil, and it dries quickly and permanently.

This makes it a great choice for artists who like to paint a landscape on site – unlike a fresh oil painting, you don't have to worry about transporting an acrylic painting without smearing the paint because it will be dry so quickly.

Pastel techniques

This is often described as a drawing medium because of the way in which the pastels are applied, yet once smudged and blended the finished result is often more like a painting which is why it is covered in this book. As you can see from the works included here, once mastered, pastel is a fabulous medium capable of capturing immense detail and subtlety of colour.

Mixed media

Artists who use a range of mediums in one painting can take advantage of the good qualities of each and can express their art in so many more ways. Acrylic, gouache and watercolour all make a good basis for a mixed-media painting, with additions of the other mediums mentioned plus pastel, pen and ink and even crayon or coloured pencil. Oils are not often used in mixed-media paintings because the others are generally water-based and therefore combine better with each other.

water colour

LANDSCAPE **WATERCOLOUR**

'I am inspired by places that feed my dreams.'

"Landscape is my language. I am drawn to places that take my breath away. Not always the grandest vistas or the highest peaks, but the configuration of forms and shapes, colours, detail and movement that compel me to paint. I am inspired by places that feed my dreams, that awaken my memories, and which remind me that I was born in Africa."

"I hear music when I sit in or pass through a place and know that this comes from some deep well inside me. I hear whole symphonies, a musical notation of the rhythm of life, with all the density, repetition and quiet pauses, with all the drama and routine. I am influenced by the Mozart I love and the Heavy Metal I'm not sure of. I am influenced by the poetry I read for pleasure and the news I read in pain. I absorb most of the art that I see and am affected by it whatever its emphasis."

"Landscape is an incredible language. It is infinite, always teaching me new things about myself and my relationship with the world. It stimulates in me an awareness and appreciation of the sacredness found in the moment and in the place."

'Rochas 13.5' by Thirza Kotzen watercolour on paper **21 x 21cm.**

Rochas 13.5.97   Thirza Kotzen.

Composition

"I am constantly aware when I am painting that the image I am creating is two-dimensional, not a 'photographic' interpretation of what I see. It is important therefore to stress the elements that capture the feelings I want to express and this may involve exaggeration, distortion and always a strength of design that acknowledges the format. The geometry of a composition is essential to make the painting work."

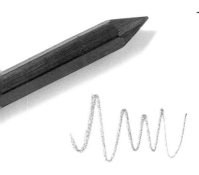

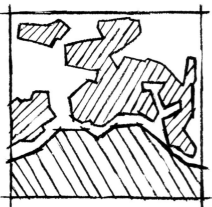

The square format, giving as much space vertically as horizontally, encourages the eyes of the viewers to rove about the picture plane in circular motions, keeping them ever interested.

Rochas 13.5.97   Thirza Kotzen.

"'Rochas 13.5' is not about a journey. It is about the magic of place that seems to be inanimate, but actually breathes with a sense of ages past. Here it is important to hold the viewer with the coherence of the moment. I came upon this place with its monumental, ancient rocks, the seasonal trees and the blood-red earth worked by man, and felt an overwhelming sense of integration and harmony. I capture this by using a square format so that one moves slowly around and around its centrifugal composition."

Notice how our eyes are drawn by recurring colours such as the acidic lime green and lush viridian. This helps to ensure our continued interest as well as helping to create colour harmony and balance.

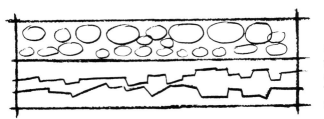

It might be easy to read a long horizontal format in the same way as a book, from left to right. To prevent the viewers' attention from passing through and then out of her painting, Thirza applies colour so it dances between and among the trees, drawing the viewers in and holding their attention.

"In 'River II' I have heightened the colour to enhance the sense of warmth and light and rhythm of the place. I have removed unimportant details and concentrated on the 'journey', the feeling of movement and the sense of time as one moves along the river. To do this I have used an elongated horizontal format. To prevent the viewer from travelling from left to right and then out of the picture, I have allowed recurring space to glow between the trees."

golden rule

Square formats

Most artists choose to paint landscapes on a 'landscape' format – that is a picture area that is wider than it is high. This not only gives maximum space to the landscape but it also conforms to our field of view which is a wide oval. The square format is rarely used but it is preferred by some artists (and photographers) because it creates a balanced image and reminds us that this is art and not simply an imitation of Nature.

Colour

"I have often been asked about my use of colour and cannot truthfully say how or why I use it. It is that part of me that comes from deep within and has a force that is both mysterious and intangible. It is the most emotional part of my creativity and I greatly value my intuitive sense about it. I intensify what I paint with the power of colour and this gives my work its cohesion and its distinctive look."

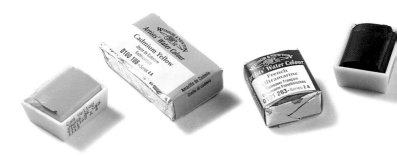

The artist's palette

"I use the best-quality materials that I can afford to buy. The purer the pigment, the more expensive the paint. I use Winsor & Newton and Old Holland watercolours and Old Holland and Rembrandt (which is very creamy) oil paint. I use a lot of ultramarine and lemon yellow and cadmium red and madders, and for the darks I always use Payne's grey, seldom black. Black can be too deadening."

lemon yellow   rose madder

rose madder   ultramarine

lemon yellow   cadmium red

ultramarine   lemon yellow

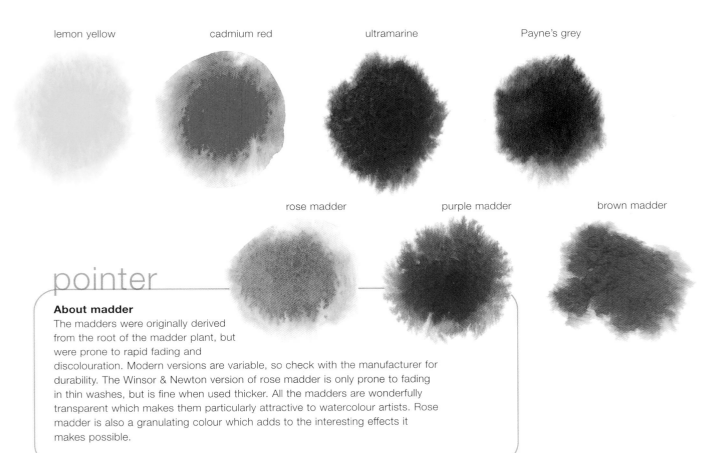

lemon yellow

cadmium red

ultramarine

Payne's grey

rose madder

purple madder

brown madder

pointer

About madder

The madders were originally derived
from the root of the madder plant, but
were prone to rapid fading and
discolouration. Modern versions are variable, so check with the manufacturer for
durability. The Winsor & Newton version of rose madder is only prone to fading
in thin washes, but is fine when used thicker. All the madders are wonderfully
transparent which makes them particularly attractive to watercolour artists. Rose
madder is also a granulating colour which adds to the interesting effects it
makes possible.

Artist's Own Technique

"I feel that technique is important but unless it is the subject matter of the work it should not be over emphasised. Proficiency comes from long-term seeing and doing. If too much stress is placed on technique the viewer is often left unmoved by the work, albeit admiring of it. I endeavour in my paintings not to straighten out their vulnerability with correctness. It is crucial to me that the viewer senses the creator, the person behind the work."

"I do not cultivate the use of any special techniques though I am sure the way I work is unique. I regard my method of painting as the means to achieve the expression and the impact that I want and it may be as simple or as complicated as necessary. In both my watercolours and oil paintings layers of paint are built up then broken down repetitively until the desired balance is attained. I am ever mindful of great artists like Picasso who achieved maximum impact and sensitivity often by the simplest means."

Thirza applies the paint rapidly, letting intuition and feeling influence the painting process so that the paint recreates her joy and delight at the scene.

shortcuts

Painting with feeling
Painting with the heart often involves pushing learnt conventions to the back of the artist's mind. But experience is never totally abandoned. Knowledge of colour balance and composition is allowed to work subconsciously to ensure an effective image, while the artist urgently responds to the view, the feel of the paint and the movement of the brush on the paper.

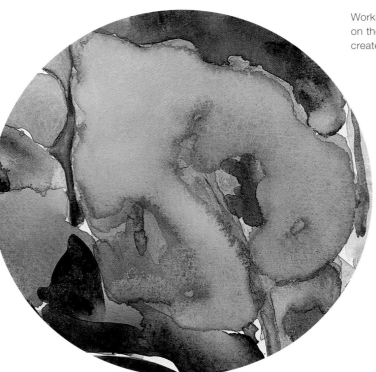

Working wet-in-wet, Thirza lets colours flow on the paper, spreading and mingling to create imaginative shapes and fresh colours.

'It is crucial to me that the viewer senses the creator, the person behind the work.'

Rochas 13.5.97   Thirza Kotzan.

By leaving white spaces between areas of colour, Thirza allows the painting to breathe and prevents the strong colours she uses from becoming overpowering.

LANDSCAPE WATERCOLOUR

"There is something beautifully serene and yet threatening about the rainforest, twisting and dense, where I spent a month painting from the field station of the Iwokrama Rainforest Research Programme on the Essiquibo River in Guyana. I had spent a month here the year before, and wanted to return. Here you can sit without a person in sight but with teeming life all around."

"While painting from the Iwokrama research station I was taken up river to this peaceful spot, surrounded by towering trees and the sounds of macaws and howler monkeys. The boatman came back for me at dusk. The area is pristine, the sand red, and a giant turtle had made her way up the bank to dig a hole for her eggs."

'The Iwokrama Rainforest, Amazon Basin' by Shirley Felts watercolour on paper **46 x 56cm.**

Composition

"Although I select my viewpoint carefully, with the best possible composition in mind, I also edit what is in view. I paint what excites me, but I do set out to find it." Even surrounded by all the lush beauty of a rainforest, Shirley still took time to select the most pleasing viewpoint. In the end she chose to paint a small clearing where a gap in the tree canopy allowed plenty of light to filter down to the rich red earth. This clearing is important in the painting, because without a break in the vegetation the scene would have no real focal point and the eyes would have no place to rest from the busy activity of the leaf shapes. "Painting in the rainforest was particularly difficult – I thought wonderful – such abundance and confusion."

'I focus on one thing, edit and build around it.'

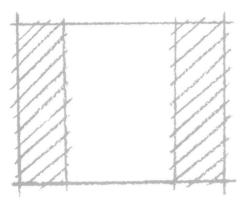

The tranquillity of the scene is enhanced by the symmetry of the composition – not only do the side borders of vegetation seem twinned, but the patch of blue sky at the top is reflected by the open ground at the bottom.

Shirley ensures our eyes are trapped within the painting and cannot leave by 'fencing them in' at the sides with the lush vegetation.

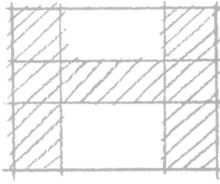

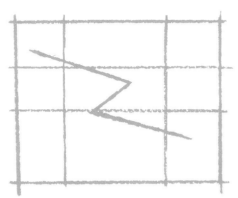

Our eyes are drawn along the diagonal gully into the depths of the painting, and are then attracted to the large palm almost at the centre whose form in turn echoes the leaf shapes in the foreground. By keeping our eyes circulating in this manner, the painting retains our interest.

golden rule

Symmetry

A symmetrical composition produces a balanced, harmonious and therefore restful image, but this format should be selected with care because if a scene is too symmetrical it may appear static and dull. Shirley has avoided this potential problem by choosing a composition which is not perfectly symmetrical. The areas of sky and land are not exactly matched and the enclosing vegetation at the sides is varied and interesting.

Colour

 Dense undergrowth is a difficult subject to attempt because of the problems of definition amongst all the mass of green. Shirley successfully overcomes this by placing light tones against dark, dark against light, a device known as counterpoint. Sometimes she lets the white of the paper show through to create the effect of flickering light, elsewhere she simply overlays paint to place deep, inky greens against lighter, warmer ones. Warmer colours tend to advance while cooler ones recede, so Shirley has painted foreground leaves in greens warmed with a little yellow or burnt sienna, and cooled the distant areas with a little ultramarine – whether they actually looked that way at the time or not.

The artist's palette

Shirley uses a limited palette, favouring plenty of sap green, ultramarine, alizarin crimson and burnt sienna.

cadmium yellow

vermilion

alizarin crimson

ultramarine

burnt sienna

sap green

sap green   ultramarine   sap green   cadmium yellow   burnt sienna   alizarin crimson

pointer

Tonal variation

In a painting like this, tonal variation is particularly important, both to suggest depth in the undergrowth and to create a lively and interesting effect. In general, because of the effects of aerial perspective, distant regions appear lighter, but where undergrowth is concerned it is the dark tones which punch through to the depths.

Artist's Own Technique

Shirley paints in the traditional style, wet-on-dry, leaving one wash of paint to dry before applying another – in the intense heat of the rainforest it would be very difficult to paint any other way, though she does manage a little wet-in-wet work in the undergrowth to suggest hazy light filtering through. She makes great use of a No. 4 series 7 Winsor & Newton sable brush, using the very tip for fine details, such as the narrow leaves of the palms, and pressing harder on the brush to splay out the head when painting larger areas such as sky and earth.

shortcuts

Working wet-in-wet

This means exactly what it says – applying wet paint on top of wet paint or paper. It creates wonderfully soft washes of colour which run, blend, spread and fade to create all sorts of misty effects and produce fabulous new colours. It's not particularly controllable because you can't tell what will happen, though this is also part of its charm, and it's best not to over use it because it can leave a picture looking formless and undefined. Because of the amount of water involved the paper should be stretched unless it is very thick – Shirley used very heavy NOT Arches paper.

As Shirley builds up colours by overlaying washes wet-on-dry, she is careful not to overwork the painting – some areas have only a hint of colour, while others have successive washes of the same colour to create great tonal depth and variation.

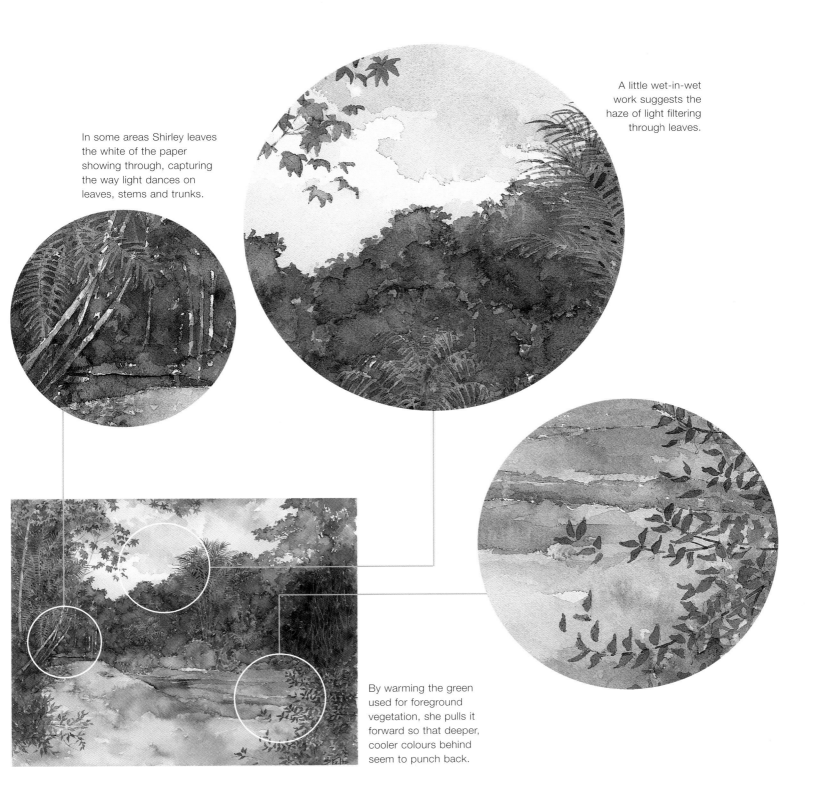

In some areas Shirley leaves the white of the paper showing through, capturing the way light dances on leaves, stems and trunks.

A little wet-in-wet work suggests the haze of light filtering through leaves.

By warming the green used for foreground vegetation, she pulls it forward so that deeper, cooler colours behind seem to punch back.

LANDSCAPE WATERCOLOUR

Salliann Putman is interested by "the pattern of the landscape, its texture and its colour," and these elements, along with her emotional response to the landscape, are explored in her paintings. She is essentially an intuitive painter. Once she gets started "the work just happens" and she finds that if she seeks certain qualities too deliberately "then the work looks static and dead". Like most good artists, her work is always moving on, "so what I say today may not always apply; my aim is always to keep my options open".

'Last Light, Tuscany' was one of a series of paintings resulting from a trip to the region. "The landscape was very inspiring, and it was at the end of the first day's painting, when the light had almost gone, that I found my subject. There was a shaft of light from the sun's final rays that caught my attention. All the other shapes seemed to diminish by comparison. I made a number of 'Last Light' paintings and in some forms seemed almost to dissolve into deep, close-toned colour."

'Last Light, Tuscany' by Salliann Putman ARWS watercolour and bodycolour **25.5 x 25.5cm.**

Composition

Salliann often plots very high horizons in her paintings, as in this one. She puts this down to the fact that she was brought up in London, England, and, like many city dwellers, consequently feels uncomfortable in vast open spaces. Her high horizons provide the same sense of enclosure as the high skylines created by office buildings and other tall structures in cities.

'I am above all an intuitive painter rather than an intellectual one.'

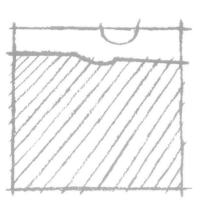

Most landscape artists place the horizon on the thirds, either one-third or two-thirds of the way down the picture area. However, experienced artists will often break this 'rule' (and others) to create striking effects. Here, the horizon is just one-seventh of the way down from the top of the picture area, so that only a strip of sky is included; even the setting sun is partially cropped at the top, adding to the sense of enclosure and bringing the eye back down to the pattern of the landscape.

Just as the darkening sky seems to press down from the top of the painting so also the mid and dark tones at the sides of the painting press in, constraining the brighter shaft of light in the centre. The vertical forms of the trees on the left and the partially cropped fields on the right stand firm to ensure that the viewers' eyes constantly return to the focus of the picture – the last light – in the centre.

golden rule

The importance of tone

Salliann uses tone to help focus attention on the heart of her painting. Capturing tonal variations, as well as colour, is fundamental to good painting, particularly if you want to focus on the pattern of the landscape – study a black-and-white landscape photo and you'll realise how important these tonal variations are. To help clarify the different tonal areas in a scene or painting, try squinting at it. What appear to be subtle gradations of tone now form into distinct areas. You'll find this helps with all your drawing and painting, whether your subject is a landscape or something else.

Colour

"Colour is of great importance to me, and in the studio I can be free to orchestrate or transpose it in any way I wish." Salliann's palette is never fixed but depends on what the subject and her feelings for it dictate. In this painting she uses the earth colours plus the madders and a range of blues. She also uses Chinese white with transparent watercolour to add body.

The artist's palette

For this painting Salliann's palette would have included brown madder, raw sienna, yellow ochre, light red, indigo, lemon yellow, cerulean blue and Chinese white. Notice the heavy bias towards the earth colours, which Salliann 'felt' were appropriate for this subject. Her lighter blue, cerulean, is a lively choice. Its greenish tint is ideal for a Mediterranean sea or sky, and in a mix it tends to have a brighter effect than, say, ultramarine. Indigo, on the other hand, is a deep inky blue, the colour of night skies. Her only red, light red, is a reliable earthy red – many reds are prone to serious fading but this earth colour isn't.

'Colour for me is feeling; every painting is different.'

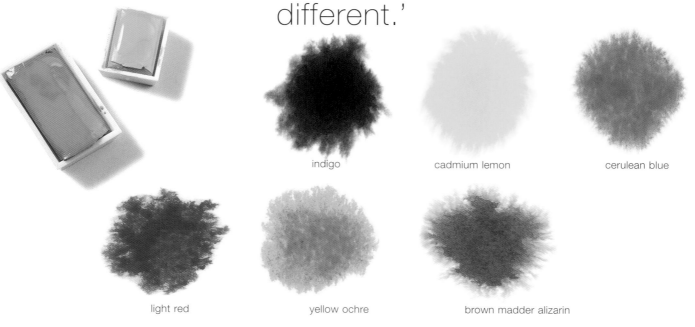

indigo

cadmium lemon

cerulean blue

light red

yellow ochre

brown madder alizarin

Salliann's specific colour choice may not have much to do with the exact colours of Nature. "It often has little to do with observed colour; it may be chosen because it adds to the mood of the subject or it may be a response to the needs of the painting." In this painting, for example, she chose a deep red for the sky. This was partly because the landscape seemed to be dissolving into the reddening last light of the sun, but also because she had been painting all day and was very hot. "The red for the sky felt right." The ochre grew from her observations, "but its placement just happened".

The earth colours

Earth colours are naturally occurring mineral pigments from clays, rocks and earths. Most have good tinting and covering power. They are traditional colours and were used in cave paintings dating back thousands of years. These pigments have a natural beauty and warm, natural tone yet are readily available and relatively inexpensive. They include the ochres which come from clays tinted by iron oxide; the umbers which are a darker range of naturally occurring clays; brown earths such as Vandyke brown and Cassel earth which owe their colour to their content of decayed organic matter; and terre verte (green earth), a soft, light but weak green which comes from green clay. Some of these pigments can be heated to change the iron and enrich the colour. Venetian red, burnt sienna and burnt umber are examples.

indigo   cadmium lemon

light red   cadmium lemon

pointer

The emotion of colour

Anyone who has anything to do with colour, be they an artist, designer or interior decorator, will tell you that colours are emotionally evocative. To an extent everyone's response is personal and based on previous associations, but generally people find blue and green soothing, violet contemplative, yellow energising and red warm, bold, vigorous or even aggressive. Muted colours are more complicated but tend to induce quieter emotions.

Artist's Own Technique

Salliann finds it better to make quick studies or drawings on site and then return to the studio where she can freely interpret the various elements that first inspired her. In the studio she can start afresh and work in any way she wishes, whereas on site, although filled with inspiration, she can "become weakened by continual looking" or in the words of the great French painter Pierre Bonnard feel "weak in front of Nature".

She likes to combine mediums to take advantage of the transparency of watercolour and the opacity of gouache as this "extends the vocabulary of the medium". She also used collage in this painting for the two trees on the left, gluing on painted tissue paper to add to the surface interest of the painting which is composed largely of transparent layers of watercolour and the more textured areas of gouache. Salliann doesn't usually seek to create texture but here "it just seemed right for the painting and what I was trying to say about the subject. In general I rely on brushwork to give interest to the marks. I may, if necessary, use other means of creating surface interest, but I don't have a fixed vocabulary of effects."

Her choice of brush is varied – she uses some sable, some mixed fibres, hog-hair brushes and varnishing brushes, "in fact, any brush which will do the job required". She works quickly "this is my natural speed; if I force myself to slow down and 'think' then often the painting fails".

shortcuts

Adding body

Artists often add a little soap or gum arabic to their paint to provide additional texture. Both give the paint extra body so that brushmarks show up better. Soap often forms tiny bubbles which dry to leave open rings or dots which can work well when capturing the texture of rock or foliage. Gum arabic dries to a shine which is helpful for reviving colours and adding richness.

'I will use any means available to me to achieve what I am after in a painting.'

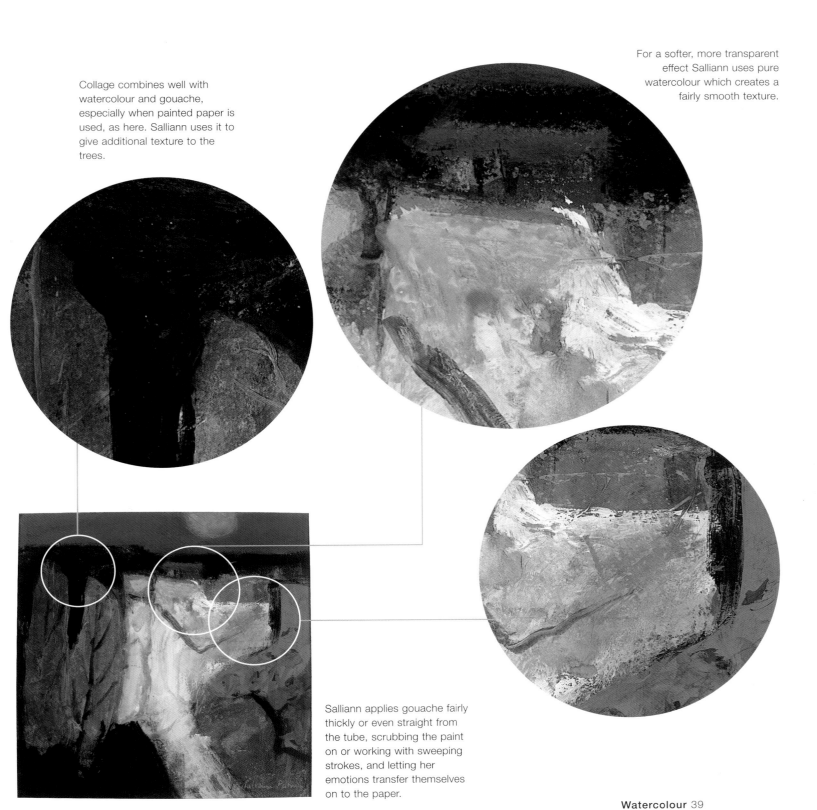

Collage combines well with watercolour and gouache, especially when painted paper is used, as here. Salliann uses it to give additional texture to the trees.

For a softer, more transparent effect Salliann uses pure watercolour which creates a fairly smooth texture.

Salliann applies gouache fairly thickly or even straight from the tube, scrubbing the paint on or working with sweeping strokes, and letting her emotions transfer themselves on to the paper.

LANDSCAPE WATERCOLOUR

"I was on my way to Rome via Abruzzo where I wanted to explore the mountains, but without a car I was stuck in a hostel beside a lake. Luckily, there was a small hill town just two miles away and I loved the steep narrow streets, the odour of damp stone and the glimpses of bright geraniums in the windows. I spent a day painting this, just below the town, sitting on a chair brought to me by a local lady. I finished it just as the sky darkened and it began to rain."

'Bomba, Abruzzo' by Katy Ellis watercolour on paper **30 x 38cm.**

20. AUG '97
BOMBA, ABRUZZO.
THUNDERY CLOUDS OVER-
HEAD + FRESH MOUNTAIN
AIR. *Ken Ould*

Composition

Katy took her time finding the best possible viewpoint to enable her to reveal the character of this hilltop town and at the same time produce a balanced image. From here the weathered houses, clustered closely around the steep, narrow streets look as if they are built on top of one another. "I walked all round searching for a good view before deciding that this was the most dramatic. Looking up from below with the hint of mountains in the background it looked most impressive."

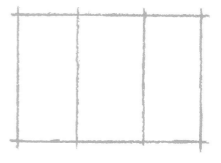

The dramatic diagonal of the hillside on the right-hand side, with its dense covering of houses, leads the eye forcefully up to the focal spire. On the left, the gentle slope also draws the eye but at a more leisurely pace. Even the tree trunks in the foreground seem to point towards the spire.

Katy positioned the focal church spire roughly a third of the way over from the left-hand side – a position usually considered most pleasing in a painting.

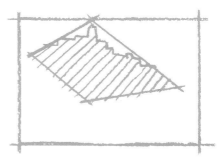

The town fills the page almost to bursting, as if the top of the spire and the edges of the town are reaching out to the edges of their domain. This makes the town seem far more imposing than if Katy had allowed more of the background to encroach on the scene.

golden rule

Cropping for drama

Katy's town exactly fills the space available, making the best use of the picture area and showing the truth of the phrase that 'what you leave out is as important as what you keep in'. Sometimes it's possible to create even more impact – and add life and movement to a painting – by actually cropping out part of the subject, a technique favoured by Impressionist Edgar Degas (1834–1917) and also used by Claude Monet (1840–1926). This can add to the intimacy of a scene or make the subject seem so powerful and impressive that it has burst beyond the onlooker's field of view.

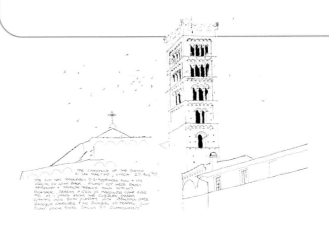

Katy's sketchbook is like a journal, with sketches accompanied by written descriptions of the atmosphere, her mood, what she was doing at the time and sometimes also describing the colours. Her written notes are invaluable, helping her recall the true sense of the place and her reaction to it when she comes to make a painting.

alizarin crimson   cadmium red   sap green   ultramarine

   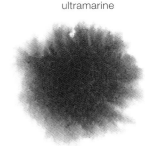

Colour

Katy tends to paint on the move, so it makes good sense for her to use a limited palette which cuts down on the amount of equipment she has to carry, although she sometimes needs to take good stocks as fresh supplies are not always readily available. A limited palette is also an advantage because it makes it easier to get to know the colours thoroughly and cuts down on time wasted trying to mix a particular shade or hue using unfamiliar colours.

Katy also uses limited equipment – a No. 4 series 7 Winsor & Newton sable brush and 150lb hot-pressed Saunders watercolour paper. She transports her watercolours and drawings in a large plastic tube which she can carry on her shoulder, and stores her watercolours, brushes, pens and charcoal in a lightweight container.

The artist's palette

Katy favours pale colours in her limited palette, often using sepia, sap green, cadmium yellow, cadmium red, alizarin crimson and ultramarine. Sepia and ultramarine provide the darkest tones, ensuring that there are no harsh notes in her paintings and she has chosen two reds, one warm and opaque, the other cool and transparent to give her maximum versatility. Because it had rained the day before this painting was made, colours – and smells – were stronger, so Katy overlaid washes to produce the depth of tone needed.

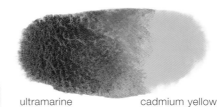

ultramarine   cadmium yellow

pointer

Hues, tones, tints and shades

Although these terms are often used indiscriminately as synonyms for 'colour', each has its own distinct meaning. Hue means the same as colour, but tone refers to a colours lightness or darkness – how it would look in a black-and-white photograph. A tint is a colour which has been lightened, while a shade is a colour which has been darkened; both refer to a colour's tone. The phrase 'shades of night' uses 'shade' correctly, because it refers to tones darkened by night.

alizarin crimson   ultramarine

sepia   cadmium yellow

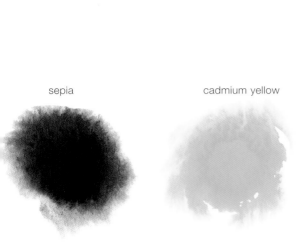

sepia   cadmium yellow

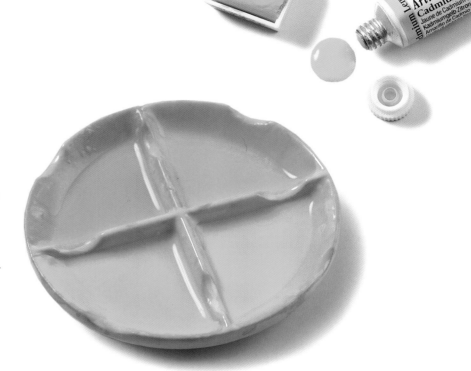

Consider cadmium yellow

There are many forms of cadmium yellow and all of them are excellent when a good brand is chosen. Cadmium yellow light is strong, bright, clean and opaque and is lightfast except in humid conditions, and the darker versions – cadmium yellow medium and cadmium yellow deep – have the same excellent qualities because they are all based on the same pigments. This also applies to cadmium lemon, a cooler, greener version. Look for the pigment PY35 or PY37 to be sure you have the genuine article. Cadmium is considered toxic, but provided you don't have the habit of sucking your brushes to shape them and use them as they are intended, this shouldn't be a problem.

'When you go out to paint, try to forget what objects you have before you: a tree, a house, a field or whatever. Merely think, here is a little square of blue, here an oblong of pink, here a streak of yellow, and paint it just as it looks to you.'
(Claude Monet)

Artist's Own Technique

When painting on site, as Katy does, it's not possible to use all the techniques available to the artist due to limited supplies (sometimes including water) and the general inconveniences of painting outside, such as battling with the forces of wind, intense heat or rain. However, through skilled handling Katy manages to use a variety of techniques to give added life to her paintings, including using a dry brush and working with pools of colour.

shortcuts

Working wet-on-dry

This term doesn't simply mean applying wet paint to dry paper. It refers to the classic watercolour technique of painting in layers, allowing the existing washes to dry before applying the next one, thus gradually building up to darker, richer areas of colour. The danger with this technique is knowing when to stop – it's easy to overwork a painting, dulling the colours by applying too many paint layers and blocking out the white of the paper.

For most areas Katy worked wet-on-dry in the classic manner to produce greater colour depth, "leaving white areas for it to breathe".

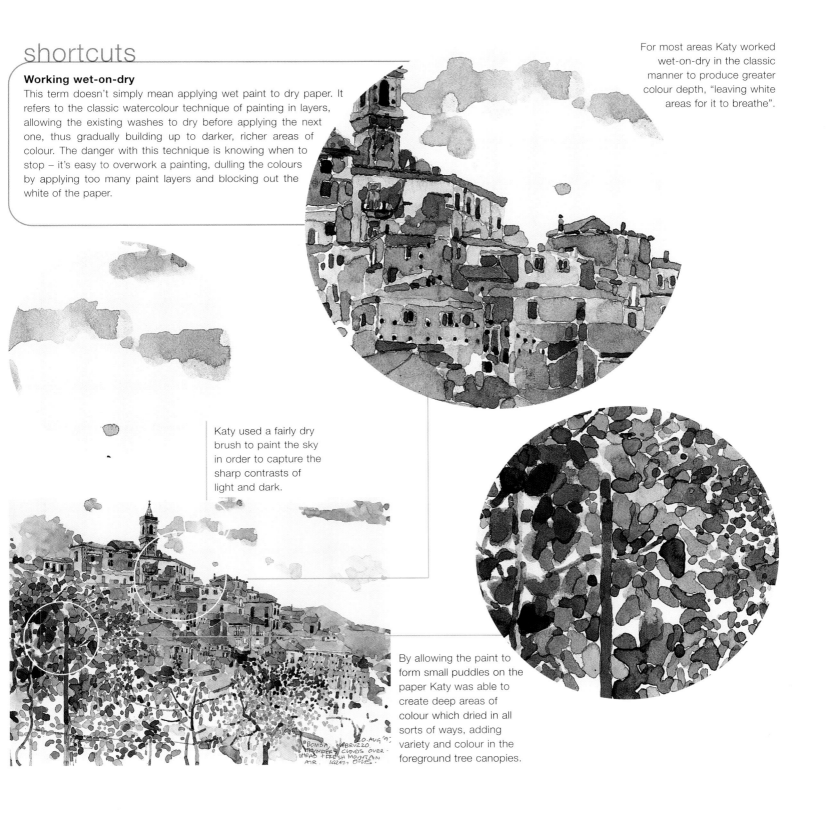

Katy used a fairly dry brush to paint the sky in order to capture the sharp contrasts of light and dark.

By allowing the paint to form small puddles on the paper Katy was able to create deep areas of colour which dried in all sorts of ways, adding variety and colour in the foreground tree canopies.

'My painting is about sensations –
not illusions but allusions.'

This is a picture about spring-time, "when on a bright and breezy day one turns, shoulder on to the wind, with colour turned up, eyes a little screwed up against the dazzle of bright light, noticing that the warmer weather is drawing up new growth."
   'First Growth' isn't a depiction of a specific place but rather a kind of emotional and visual summing up of the landscape, light and colour of a Spring day in the Pennine region in which Stephen now lives. As he says, "I wish not to make a representation of a particular place but use a place or view of a place, and especially the weather, the lighting and colour, as a starting point from which to allude to other qualities."

'First Growth' by Stephen Court gouache on paper **33 x 43.7cm.**

Composition

This composition is based on a notional viewing point from an elevated site, looking across a valley space to rising hillsides at an equal or greater altitude to that of the viewing site. "In the area where I now live, in the Pennines, this upland formation is a common feature, and one-third sky to two-thirds land seemed to suit the way I wanted to make the picture."

Stephen creates his compositions through the careful orchestration of colour and texture, playing off warm (advancing) and cool (recessive) colours, thin, smooth paint layers and thicker, more textured layers. He relates this very much to music in which "the colour relationships and textures make the pattern of the tune, and the masses make the chords and themes".

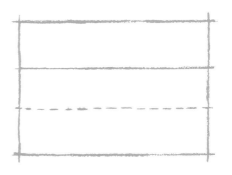

Stephen has plotted the horizon roughly two-thirds of the way up the picture area, giving plenty of room for him to express the sense of space one feels as well as sees as one looks across a valley to the hills beyond.

The strong lemon yellow paint is placed to draw the eye continuously over to the horizon. This is achieved by using the colour lightly but widely in the foreground, then intensifying it at the horizon. The splashes in the sky also seem to force the eye back down to the horizon.

golden rule

Leading the eye

If your painting is one of many in a gallery, you'll want to do something to draw attention to it. This can be done consciously, but many artists do it instinctively. Stephen uses colour to pull the viewer into his painting, a technique which works well. You can use colour lavishly, as Stephen does, or use it sparingly, setting off a small area of bright, hot colour in an otherwise cold picture, for example. You can do the same thing with line – paths, gates or the roll of a hillside can draw viewers in – or with framing, placing bushes or trees at the edges to prevent the eye from straying. If you are painting from life, simply adjust your position to take advantage of these affects which occur naturally.

'A piece starts from little more than a wish to try something out.'

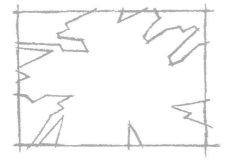

While the yellow paint skims us straight across to the far hills, the cool green and blue in the valley, which are recessive colours, seem to fall away above and below, giving us the sensation of flying over a chasm or of being drawn into the painting.

Stephen went up in a glider to take this reference photograph to aid his painting.

Colour

For Stephen, colour is inexorably linked to composition. He starts his paintings with colour, rather than in the traditional way with a pencil sketch, so that "the picture is made, or rather becomes made, firstly from a notion established from washes and areas and pieces of colour played as a sort of dance. These areas of colour are forged, refined, pushed, pulled and elaborated as the piece progresses." While he paints he holds in his mind the various things he wishes to deal with so that "the work is, as it were, driven along".

The artist's palette

Stephen used a very limited range of colours in this palette. He chose Daler Rowney and Winsor & Newton Designers' Gouache, noting that it is "a highly versatile and handy sort of paint amongst the water-soluble paints". He points to its good covering power, with relatively high pigment content "finely ground enough to obtain tints and washes". Adding gum arabic to the diluted paint, he says, "can afford lush and lustrous qualities similar to ink glazes," while used dry and pasty, gouache "gives scope for nylon or steel spatula and dry-brush handling". This enables him to lay on paint and then "drive into the surface with a favoured old 4 3/4in (12cm) hog, spatula blade or rag to steer and draw the paints".

ultramarine

sky blue

viridian

brilliant green

lemon yellow

Mars red

burnt sienna

spectrum yellow

brilliant green

sky blue

lemon yellow

burnt sienna

spectrum yellow

sky blue

ultramarine

viridian

Colour durability

Some gouache – or watercolour – paints are prone to fading, sometimes in a matter of weeks or months, sometimes over a number of years. To ensure his paintings are durable, Stephen always refers to the colour-makers' claims for lightfastness in the small range he uses and, as he says, "would not trouble with fugitives [colours which fade] or semi-durables knowingly".

The durability of a colour depends on the pigment(s) used, the quality and brand. That means that you can't always assume that a certain named colour is lightfast – different brands marketing a colour under the same name may use different pigments (see right) – so always refer carefully to the manufacturer's information charts to avoid disappointment.

Names and brands

If you run out of a favourite colour and can't find your usual brand in your local art shop, don't assume that another brand will do. Another brand's lemon yellow, for example, could be significantly lighter, warmer or more fugitive. Check the colour index number on the tubes to find the closest match to the one you want. Generally you'll find the artists' ranges contain better pigments than the more economical students' ranges.

About yellow

The first yellow pigments were obtained from a range of natural materials, some of them bizarre. Indian yellow, for example, came from the concentrated urine of cows fed on mango leaves and denied water; gamboge came from tree sap and was highly fugitive; while there was even a yellow derived from gall-stones. Today's manufactured yellows are generally more reliable, though some, such as gamboge, are not very lightfast. Naples yellow, yellow ochre and the cadmium yellows are recommended. Naples yellow contains lead, so as an alternative you can mix your own. For a warm version Stephen suggests mixing titanium white with a hint of pale yellow and burnt sienna; for a cool version add a hint of sky blue to the mix.

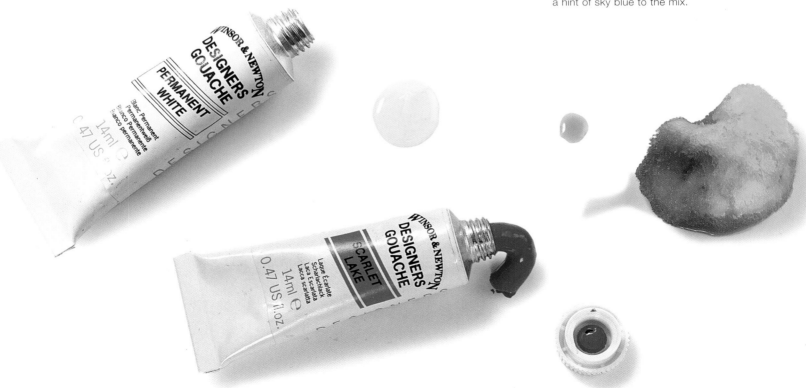

Stephen laid on washes with a fitch and small turkey sponge.

Artist's Own Technique

Stephen prepares himself mentally as well as physically for a painting. "It is well to enjoy the preparation, one's tools and materials assembled, then, taking a breath deeply and slowly, gather the idea and cast marks and shapes directly. Draw together or slice apart whole sections, mastering and massing the elements of the composition so that it sits well in its space."

In this painting he used a 3/4in (2cm) fitch and a small turkey sponge to lay the washes and to work the paint, sometimes wiping the colour with the side of his hand. In other paintings he might apply the paint fairly dry and pasty so he can use a favoured old 4 3/4in (12cm) broad-body white hog, a spatula blade or rag to steer and draw the paint "sweeping and nudging it to form the shapes around the pictorial space".

In 'Harvest Home' Stephen used gouache colours and also fine-ground pigments mixed with PVA glue medium, handling the paint with fairly large brushes, the smallest being a 3/4in (2cm) fitch, wiping with his hand, and shifting colour about with a rag. He also used spray canisters of motor paint to effect "dustings of atmospherics and modelling of spaces in the composition," a technique learned from fellow artist Denis Bowen.

'Harvest Home' by Stephen Court gouache and cellulose on paper **67 x 42.5cm.**

'A picture space is a place to play and experiment.'

In some areas Stephen used the paint fairly dry and pasty so he could steer the paint with his white hog, spatula blade or a rag.

shortcuts

Gum arabic

Gouache already contains gum arabic as a binder, but by adding a little more, as Stephen points out, you can give the paint qualities similar to ink glazes. Gum arabic can be bought in bottles and added to water when mixing paint to give it more body and to make it less runny and easy to blend. It can revive colours by enriching them and adding a slight glaze. However, it can cause cracking if used neat, and should always be mixed with a high proportion of water – experience will teach you how much.

Using spray canisters (aerosols) of motor paint enables him to reproduce the look of atmospherics.

oils

"My paintings are a compound of different elements I have seen and recorded which best express the narrative flow of ideas. However, I never intend that the metaphoric interpretations should become the main function of the work. It is important to me that the paintings are presented first and foremost as the landscapes which inspired me, in a convincing and unforced way, and that any other meaning is something that will gradually leak out of the painting in time."

"'The River's Source' is part of a series of paintings on the cycle of the water course from stream to river to sea to ocean and back through cloud and rain. My initial inspiration came from a few lines in a poem by Sorley MacLean called 'The Woods of Raasay' [see below], a long and rambling poem in which the landscape is a metaphor for life in all its uncertainty. In my series I too reflect the unpredictability of our lives between the certainty of birth and of death."

'The River's Source' by Philip Braham oil on canvas **137 x 178cm.**

'O the wood, O the wood!
　the aspect of pleasant beauty,
　of the eye that is soft and bright,
　the lively jewel in blindness.

The way of the sap is brown,
　oozing up to its work,
　the wine that is always new and living
　unconscious, untaught.

There is no knowledge of the course
　of the crooked veering of the heart,
　and there is no knowledge of the damage
　to which its aim unwittingly comes.

There is no knowledge, no knowledge,
　of the final end of each pursuit,
　nor of the subtlety of the bends
　with which it loses its course.'

from 'The Woods of Raasay' by Sorley MacLean

Composition

"A work which relies mostly on receding horizontal planes will seem calm while diagonals intersecting will carry the eye dramatically across the surface of the work." Both paintings shown on these pages contain both these elements – horizontals for calm and diagonals for energy. This keeps the eyes always interested, yet the overall sense of calm enables quiet, deep contemplation.

Although Philip is aware of the traditional rule of thumb that a landscape should be divided on a 1/3:2/3 basis, he draws a line of misty haze across the centre of the canvas, veiling the distant scene and creating an air of mystery. This equal division seems to set up a dialogue between sky and land, spiritual and earthly matters.

"The rich green valley between the rivers represents life's abundance."

"The forest represents the idea of community; a grouping together which provides security and shelter. In the foreground the dead trees at the forest's edge are a reminder of the vulnerability of isolation."

The final composition for 'Divergent Paths' (overleaf) is directly linked to Philip's initial ink study (above) but this is not always the case (see right).

Philip used the burst of light through the clouds from this study in his painting 'The River's Source'. Together, these studies show how an artist may use studies and sketch material directly or simply as a jumping-off point.

golden rule

Aerial perspective

Minute particles of dust and moisture in the air affect how we see colours, especially those far away. Effectively they create veils over distant areas, making colours seem paler, bluer and less contrasty. Artists can give their paintings more depth by recreating this effect. One way is to apply a pale wash over the finished distant area; another option is to start painting in the far sections with pale, neutral colours, using more intense, cleaner colours as objects come closer.

Colour

Although Philip tends to use the same palette for all his work, the resulting paintings vary from soft and muted to strong and vibrant. Yet whatever the colours used, all his works retain a deep sense of spirituality and immense luminosity. His remarkable ability to capture something so tenuous as light can be put down to his skill in applying colour. One means of achieving it is by using complementaries. "I usually begin a painting in a wash of complementary colour to the final hue, and I allow some of that to show in the finished work. This allows the dominant colour to vibrate and helps to create the sense of light which is fundamental to my work."

The artist's palette

"My palette is as follows: titanium white, Payne's grey, ultramarine, Prussian blue, viridian, terre verte, raw umber, burnt sienna, Indian red, raw sienna, yellow ochre, cadmium yellow, cadmium orange and alizarin crimson. I use Winsor & Newton artist's quality paint for its consistency and durability."

'Divergent Paths' by Philip Braham oil on canvas **137 x 183cm.**

viridian   alizarin crimson

viridian   Prussian blue

alizarin crimson   ultramarine

'Colour is used to convey the emotional tone I require. Some paintings are strident while others are almost silent.'

Payne's grey

ultramarine

Prussian blue

viridian

terre verte

raw umber

burnt sienna

Indian red

raw sienna

yellow ochre

cadmium yellow

cadmium orange

alizarin crimson

'I purposely avoid using any 'tricks' in my work.'

pointer

Overlaying complementary colours

Placing complementary colours (opposites on the colour wheel) next to each other makes them seem more intense, especially if they are matched in tone and strength. If, on the other hand, you mix a little of the complementary colour into your colour, you'll 'knock it back' to create a pleasing neutral. Overlaying complementaries takes advantage of both these factors. When the top colour is transparent the two colours will mix to create soft neutrals, but where thicker colour is applied in broken areas so the undercolour is allowed to stand, you'll get all the sizzle that complementary pairs produce.

shortcuts

Gesture drawing
This has more to do with capturing the essence of something – or your reaction to it – than with photographic realism or accuracy. With grand sweeping strokes or harsh scrubbing motions the artist aims to recreate the subject with the minimum of brush or pen strokes but with maximum emotion. It is a method totally alien to Philip's quiet, meditative, caressing way of working.

Artist's Own Technique

"My painting technique is very direct – I work immediately in paint. If I use photographs for reference I work only from a contact sheet which reproduces the scene at postage-stamp size. I do that to avoid becoming caught up reproducing the details of a scene when I'm trying to capture its essence. Also the photographs are black and white for the same reason."

"I purposely avoid using any 'tricks' in my work and even eschew the temptation to use texture or gesture (see above) as these are seductive devices which often become a painting's *raison d'être*. I try to paint truthfully and quietly, and allow subtlety to carry the poetic narrative of the work."

"A painting usually takes about a month to complete, and although I might begin two or three works at the same time, I tend to push one to completion before returning to the others – I find the concentration required impossible to sustain if working simultaneously on others."

Work begins by "making sketches and taking photographs, but above all, thinking". Philip spends time every few months in the country or at the coast researching his work and clearing his mind, often taking books of poetry or philosophy that particularly inspire him. "Suddenly the landscape around me triggers new ideas and I find I'm between the worlds of outer reality and inner truth. I try to recapture that vision in my studio work."

ILFORD XP2   8

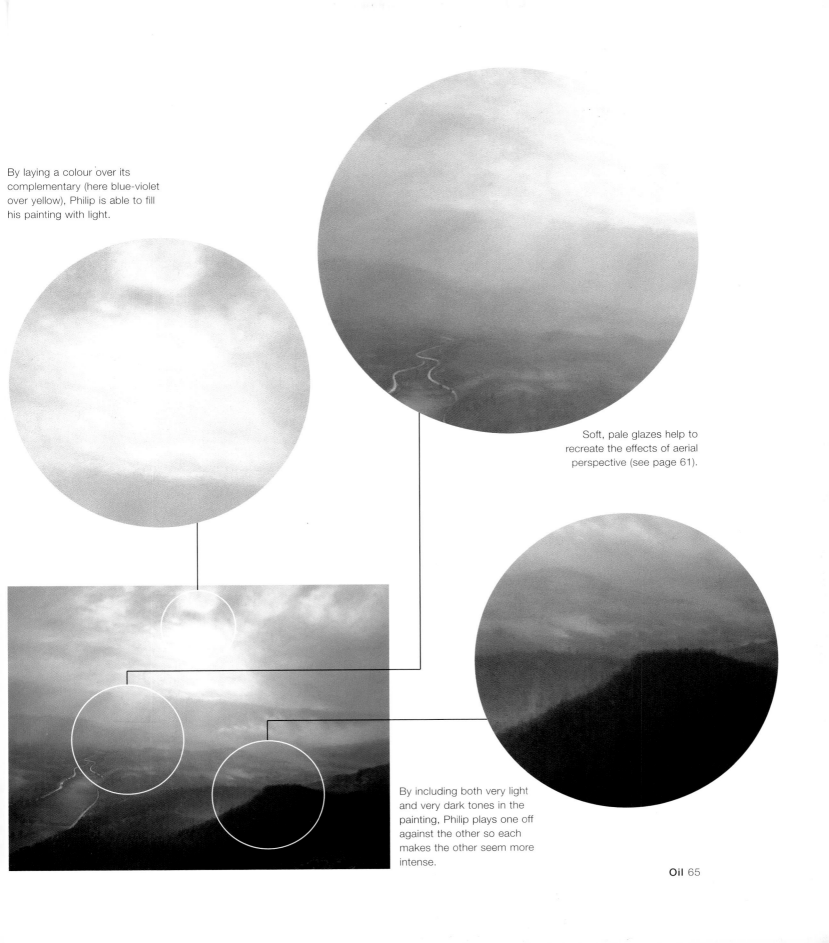

By laying a colour over its complementary (here blue-violet over yellow), Philip is able to fill his painting with light.

Soft, pale glazes help to recreate the effects of aerial perspective (see page 61).

By including both very light and very dark tones in the painting, Philip plays one off against the other so each makes the other seem more intense.

Oil 65

Light and the subtleties of colour it creates as it plays across the landscape are the constant themes of Hugh McNeil McIntyre's work. Travelling widely through much of Europe and on to Brazil, Hugh has been able to observe – and capture – the wonderful variations created by the different intensities of the sun in these regions: the warm, relaxing glow of the Mediterranean, the cooler tones of his homeland Scotland and the bright, often harsh contrasts of the Brazilian light.

In this picture Hugh captures the golden light which wafts over fields and hedges as the sun sets over the tranquil landscape of Reillanette in the region of Drôme, France. The intensity of the evening light is strengthened by the contrast with the lilac shadows in the foreground where the land is already growing cold.

'Lavender Fields, Reillanette' by Hugh McNeil McIntyre oil on canvas **81 x 81cm.**

Composition

In this landscape Hugh has concentrated on the arrangement of mouth-watering colours created by the play of evening light on the fields. He has given the landscape greater coverage in his painting than the sky – it takes up roughly two-thirds of the canvas – but the golden light that fills the sky and part of the landscape also takes up two-thirds of the picture area. The transitional area in the middle is at once both landscape and sky as the sunlight melts trees, hedges and soil into the golden sunset.

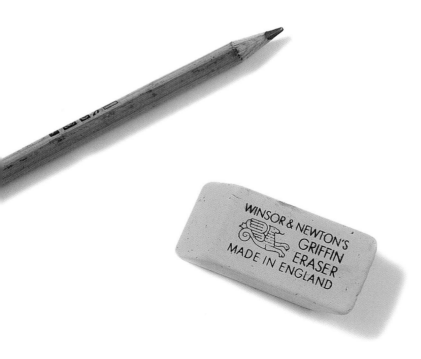

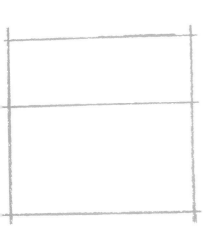

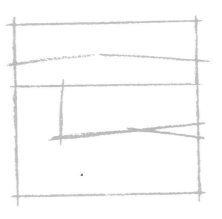

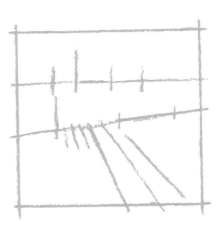

Hugh has plotted the horizon roughly two-thirds of the way up the canvas to give the landscape more prominence and to avoid the rather deadening effect that a central horizon can often produce.

Although the sky only takes up about a third of the canvas, its colours extend over the landscape, taking up nearly two-thirds of the picture area and creating a pleasing balance with the landscape.

Hugh has not only divided the canvas roughly into thirds horizontally, but vertically as well, placing one of the larger telegraph poles where these structural dividing lines intersect towards the top left.

golden rule

Finding a focus

The starting point in any composition is to decide what is going to be the main focus of attention and where to place it. In a flat landscape like this you'll find the eye is constantly drawn to the horizon, so make that your focal point. The temptation is to draw the horizon line straight across the centre of the page – don't. You'll usually get better results if you place it slightly above or below the centre line, roughly dividing the canvas into thirds.

Colour

Hugh uses colour to fill his painting with light. By using his knowledge of complementary colours he is able to bring some colours up to their maximum intensity, placing violet shadows next to patches of lemon sunlight and adding a haze of cerulean to the orange sky for maximum power and vibrancy. He also plays off near complementaries, adding splashes of orange or burgundy next to green. These increase the colour intensities without going for overkill.

The artist's palette

"To create the feeling of atmospheric warmth I mix touches of colour into my whites and into each other. Most frequently used are Naples yellow, cadmium yellow, cadmium orange, raw sienna and flesh tint. These assist in the creation of secondary and tertiary complements when used in conjunction with phthalo blue and sap green. For extreme dark tones I mix Vandyke brown with phthalo blue and sap green." Hugh also uses zinc white and for his red he favours Windsor red or cadmium light red.

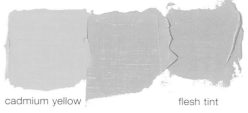

cadmium yellow   flesh tint

sap green   phthalo blue

Naples yellow   sap green

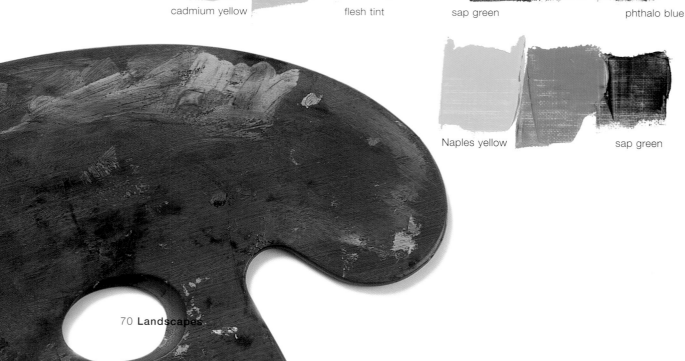

The colour wheel

The colour wheel comprises the three primaries – red, yellow and blue – with the three secondaries in between. (These artists' primary colours are not to be confused with the three primaries of light used in photography which are red, yellow and green.) Thus the colour wheel moves in sequence from red to orange, yellow, green, blue and finally violet when it completes the circle.

An extended colour wheel

The primaries – the colours from which all other colours can technically be mixed – are placed on the colour wheel first. Between them are the secondaries, mixed from the two adjacent primaries in equal quantities. By mixing each secondary with the adjacent primary in equal quantities you'll get a tertiary colour. You can continue this process to mix many more variations, but you'll find that this simple colour wheel is the most useful as it is easy to remember and to visualize.

pointer

Complementary colours

Complementary colours are those colours directly opposite each other on the colour wheel which, when laid side by side increase each other's power and intensity. Thus orange placed next to blue' or red next to green' seem almost to sizzle and vibrate. Artists often put a touch of the complementary colour into an object's shadow to brighten areas which can otherwise look quite dull and to increase the intensity of the object.

Naples yellow

cadmium yellow

flesh tint

sap green

phthalo blue

cadmium red

cadmium light red

Winsor red

Vandyke brown

Artist's Own Technique

Hugh applies paint enthusiastically, using any tool that will do the job including knives, brushes and cloths. He uses good quality paints and knives but because his brushes take quite a bashing he never spends much money on them, buying the cheapest ones he can find in his local supermarket or charity shop – his only good brushes are given to him at Christmas or for birthdays.

'I put paint on with anything I can find – my hands, bits of old towels, brushes, knives, whatever.'

Hugh starts by roughing in the composition with flat brushes. Then he might cut out with knives and put paint on using whatever tools seem appropriate. Notice that in some areas he scrubs or smears on the paint quite thickly while in others he applies the lightest of dry-brush strokes or scrapes colour off to leave a mere trace of colour. This creates a variety of textures which contributes to the liveliness of the painting.

"I often turn the canvas through 90 or 180 degrees to avoid directional brushwork and to maintain a fresh eye on the work. I work in fairly intense bursts, doing up to seven canvasses at a time. When I reach the point of hesitation on what to do next, I remove the work and replace it with another. By doing this I avoid overworking passages and maintain a fresh eye without wasting time staring at a canvas waiting for inspiration. I also try to work on several contrasting subjects at any time so that each change of canvas is a new start, from urban architecture to mountain landscape or harbour scene; from morning light to top-lit midday or evening glow, always varied, always fresh. Studio work is done at night between 10pm and 6am. At these times I get total peace to concentrate on the work. The phone doesn't ring and no friends drop in for a chat. It humbles me to think what Rembrandt, Turner or any of the other greats might have achieved with central heating and electric light."

shortcuts

Get the composition right

It's easy for an artist to get carried away with the application of colour in the early stages of a painting, only to step back and see that although there are some wonderful textures, the composition is flawed. The artist then has no recourse but to wipe off areas of the painting and start again. To avoid this, experienced artists always begin with a light application of paint which allows overpainting and correction of errors. Once the composition is right it's time to have lots of fun freely creating texture.

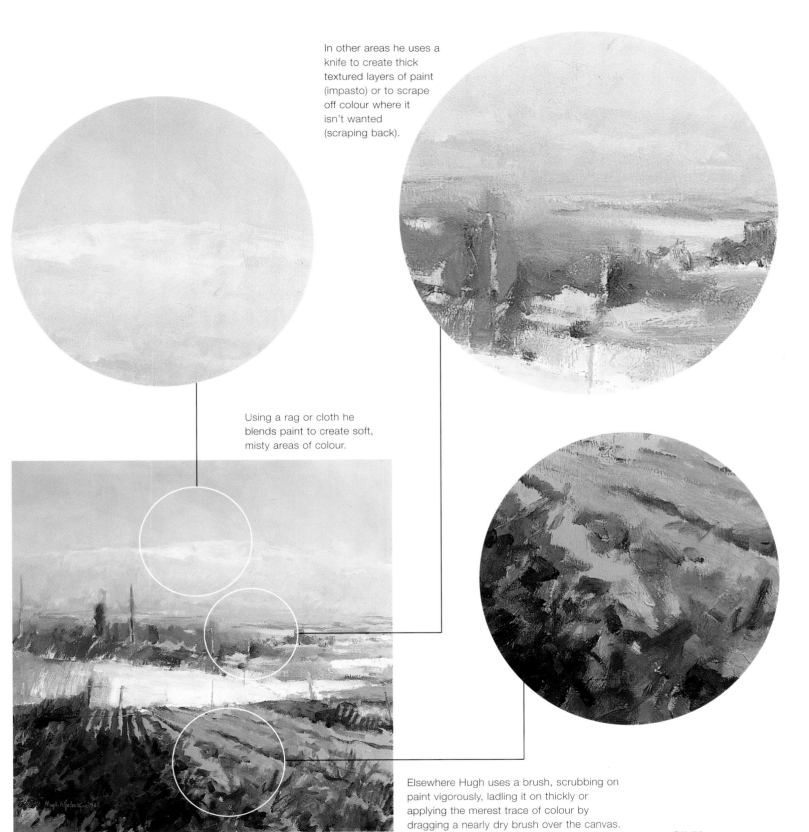

In other areas he uses a knife to create thick textured layers of paint (impasto) or to scrape off colour where it isn't wanted (scraping back).

Using a rag or cloth he blends paint to create soft, misty areas of colour.

Elsewhere Hugh uses a brush, scrubbing on paint vigorously, ladling it on thickly or applying the merest trace of colour by dragging a nearly dry brush over the canvas.

LANDSCAPES OILS

"I go to the South of France to paint and work around a little village called Vieussan along the river Orb, north from Béziers. One day I went a little further afield and came across this view as I reached the top of a hill. It was a little hamlet surrounded by a patchwork of criss-cross vineyards. It was a clear, blue-skied day and the colours were extremely vivid. Across the valley I could hear the voices of people in the hamlet – children shouting, even plates clattering as people had their lunch outside. When I look at the work I still hear the sounds and recall everything."

opposite **'Vineyards at Bérlou'** oil on canvas **61 x 61cm.**
left **'Laurel'** oil on canvas **41 x 41cm.**

by Andrew Walker

Composition

"Nowadays as I go around looking at the world I am continuously squaring-off pieces of Nature, composing paintings in my mind's eye. I was particularly excited by the small patchworks of striped fields which I depicted in 'Vineyards at Bérlou' – their geometry would break up the picture plane so well and allow for a kind of gestural mark-making that I enjoy."

Andrew was first attracted by the patchwork of fields, so he placed these at the centre of the painting, pushing the buildings into the top-left corner. Even in this position we are drawn to the houses, led there by the regimented lines of the vines.

golden rule

Keeping viewers interested

One of the main features of a good painting is that it keeps the viewers constantly interested, so that it can be hung on the same wall for years but still make the owner stop in his tracks to contemplate it for a while. One of the ways of achieving this is to lead the viewer's eyes on a merry dance about the picture plane, making sure there is lots going on in all sections. The patchwork of fields featured in 'Vineyards at Bérlou' with the lines of the vines running in all directions and the activity of the village buildings, not to mention the fabulous symphony of colours, all ensure there is plenty of entertainment in this painting.

'Houses at Laurel' oil on canvas **61 x 46cm.**

Andrew has painted at Laurel, a small farm in the region, many times;"I love it as a subject with the buildings horizontal but stepping down and the vertical pine trees. The hills at the back rise up steeply, so if you zoom in for your composition there is no sky – just buildings surrounded by dense, sweeping colour."

Andrew has placed the houses – the focus of the painting – on the Golden Section (see page 9), roughly where the lines dividing the painting into thirds intersect. This is considered a key position in any composition and was regarded as such even in Renaissance times when compositional geniuses such as Piero della Francesca (1420–92) approached the subject with mathematical precision.

When Andrew painted the scene again, he worked from a slightly different angle and focused in on the buildings even more tightly, filling the canvas with an explosion of colour and intensifying its emotional power.

'I love the idea when I'm back in Scotland that my subjects are just sitting, waiting for me. It's good to be away and then return with revived excitement for them.'

Colour

"Colour is very important to me for its emotional value and I try to maximise the intensity of the colours I use. You have to increase the pitch, gradually building up the music the colour makes, creating harmonies and chords – it's an orchestral thing. One can go too far and so you have to bring it down a little to create a balance and greater unity. All parts of the painting need to be playing the same key, as it were."

"My paintings tend to begin with very different colours to the final result. I like to start by pushing the thing way out of control so I have to bring it back. Layers of colour and density result. I do a lot of colour mixing on the actual painting. The colours beneath colours are very important to me, and the resulting texture too."

"There is a lot of colour theory about but after many years of using colour I am now actively trying to know less about it and trust to my feelings for it. One can look and look but eventually you have to feel it."

"In this painting one can really see the foundation of colours coming through. That's the thing about Mediterranean light – objects are made up of layers of colour; shadows are blue and green and purple. It shows so readily with the Impressionists and Bonnard when they were working down there."

lemon yellow   cadmium orange

cobalt violet   cobalt blue

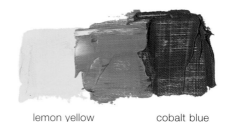

lemon yellow   cobalt blue

The artist's palette

Andrew uses Winsor & Newton paints. He has a reasonably large palette but may not use all of the colours in a painting, and he never uses black. His palette includes many of the highly reliable cadmium hues, a violet, three blues, three greens and just two earth colours – burnt sienna and yellow ochre. This enables him to create a high colour key: a large palette helps reduce the amount of mixing which can dull the colours, and those that he has chosen have brilliant depth and colour clarity, especially the cadmiums which, being of the same family, mix wonderfully well with each other. The minimal use of earth colours, which tend to be muted, also helps keep the colours bright.

burnt sienna

yellow ochre

lemon yellow

cadmium yellow

cadmium orange

cadmium red

cadmium red deep

cobalt violet

pointer

Colours sold as 'hues'

Paints labelled 'hue', such as cadmium yellow hue tend to be a lot cheaper than the real thing (cadmium yellow). This is because they are imitations of the true colours and are not made from the same pigments. It may therefore mean they are not as reliable. Before buying a paint labelled as a hue always check its properties with the manufacturer and if in any doubt spend the extra money on the real thing. Be warned, though, just because a paint has the proper name is no guarantee that it is the real thing – stick with tried and tested brands.

cerulean

cobalt blue

ultramarine

viridian

oxide of chromium

emerald green

Artist's Own Technique

"I spend the majority of my time working outdoors on landscapes throughout the year. I find energy in the fresh air, the wind, the constant changes of light, the heat or the cold. Some paintings take several seasons to complete – I may have to wait twelve months for snow to return or for a particular field to be sown with a crop of barley."

Andrew doesn't usually make preliminary drawings or sketches any more but paints on site, travelling in his car with a variety of canvases together with his paints and portable easel. "I like to put all the enthusiasm and feeling I have for the subject into the actual work itself. Somehow doing an initial drawing would dilute that energy. I prefer the emotion to build up so that I work quite quickly and concentratedly."

For variety and textural interest Andrew uses a selection of brushes – mainly hogs' hair bristle brushes, both flat and round. "I particularly like flat brushes because they provide a broad or narrow edge option which gives variability in one movement – it suits the way I work." He also sometimes uses decorator's brushes of 1/2, 1 and 2in wide. "They are good for dragging paint, building texture, stippling and laying on large quantities of paint." He doesn't use texture mediums, preferring to dilute his paints with turpentine and linseed oil.

'I don't understand why anybody would want to shut themselves up in some room. Maybe for drawing, sure; but not for painting.' (Claude Monet)

Using a fairly dry brush to scumble on the paint adds variety to his marks.

Stippling vigorously by pressing with the tip of the brush creates yet another mark and adds to the textural build-up in the painting.

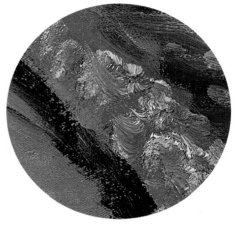

You can see how much Andrew enjoys mark-making (see page 122), as he applies the paint vigorously throughout, leaving the bold brushmarks to stand for themselves.

shortcuts

Brushmarks

Many amateur painters try to rid their work of all brushmarks in an attempt at creating realism, but thereby they also rid their painting of much of its personality – brushmarks add a sense of movement and dynamism as well as helping to create interesting textures as you can see by looking at any painting by Van Gogh. To make the brushmarks stand out more, artists can use paints fairly thickly or even undiluted or they can add a bulking medium such as those designed for impasto work. Using different brush shapes and working with a vigorous, free style also helps pep up the brushwork.

Drawn to this scene by the colours and variety in the trees on the riverbank and their contrast with the sleek fields and sleepy river, Evelyn Pottie wanted to capture the contrasts between these elements and create a real sense of their three-dimensional forms. Captivated by the great distance she could see from this viewpoint, she also wanted to convey the immensity of the vista. She chose to paint the view in late summer "with the late afternoon sun casting light from the right-hand side, and shining through the high cloud on to parts of the landscape."

This is one of Evelyn's favourite areas in the Scottish Highlands, so when commissioned to paint a landscape for an Offshore Oil-production Platform she had no hesitation in making her choice. Despite its familiarity – "sometimes I drive by and notice what it is like without stopping to draw" – she recognized its potential and has made studies of it in most seasons of the year. "It changes dramatically according to the time of day, season and the weather conditions."

'River Findhorn at Tomatin' by Evelyn Pottie oil on board **130 x 100cm.**

Composition

Working in the classical way, Evelyn makes sketches and colour notes on site and then returns to the studio to produce her paintings. She may work on a painting right away, but she might equally return to an old sketch as a basis for a new work. If a page of her sketchbook isn't big enough she'll simply stick on more paper and carry on drawing. This is a good working practice – it's better to add paper where it's needed than to try to condense everything into a space which is too small or to miss off something which may be required later in a painting. Equally, sketches don't have to fill the page if the subject doesn't warrant it.

'I will leave out whatever I please and move trees around if it suits me.'

"Back in the studio, I make a larger working drawing in which the elements of the landscape are both consciously and unconsciously placed. I often find I have used the thirds or Golden Section position for key elements of the landscape, but as I like to use as much space as possible for the land forms I often reduce the area of sky to less than a third. I think that land use – roads, animal tracks, plantations and buildings – gives a sense of place to a landscape so in that respect I am true to what I see, but I will leave out whatever I please and move trees around if it suits me."

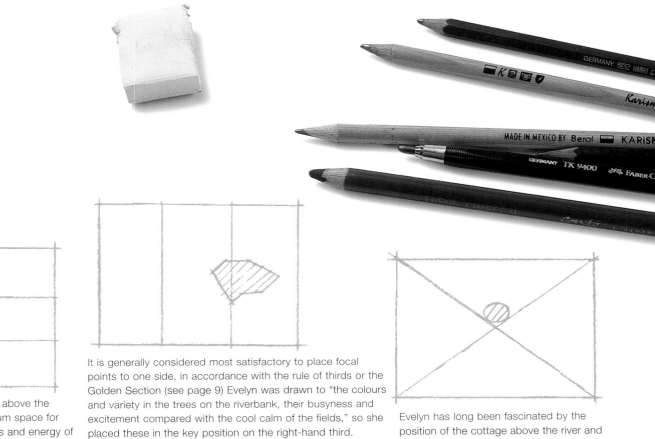

Evelyn has pushed the horizon above the 1/3:2/3 division to give maximum space for exploring the textures, contours and energy of the landscape. Notice, however, that even though the sky is given less space it is not neglected but richly painted with dramatic cloud forms.

It is generally considered most satisfactory to place focal points to one side, in accordance with the rule of thirds or the Golden Section (see page 9) Evelyn was drawn to "the colours and variety in the trees on the riverbank, their busyness and excitement compared with the cool calm of the fields," so she placed these in the key position on the right-hand third.

Evelyn has long been fascinated by the position of the cottage above the river and unconsciously placed it at the centre of the composition where it draws the eye.

golden rule

Using a viewfinder or Ls

To help find a striking composition artists sometimes look at a scene through a viewfinder (a piece of card with a rectangular window cut out of it), moving it about until it frames a satisfactory composition – a camera can be used in the same way. It helps if the window has the same proportions as the support. However, most artists include more than they need in their sketchbook material since a scene can always be cropped in the final painting. Back in the studio two L-shaped pieces of black card can help to crop the sketch, moved about until they enclose a pleasing composition.

Colour

"In the initial stages of a painting I use a restricted palette of colours to block in large areas of tone and colour, but as the painting progresses I will add others. My choice of colour is rather intuitive: I refer to my colour notes and try to remember colours I have seen, but I sometimes heighten or lighten the intensity of a colour to alter the composition or impact on the emotions."

Evelyn uses quite a large palette of colours to complete a painting, but although green is an important colour to any landscape artist, she only works with one ready-made version – viridian. This is because she prefers to mix her own greens from ochres, yellows and blues. By mixing her own greens she is able to produce much more varied and subtle colours than by sticking with ready-made versions, straight from the tube. Her soft, mixed greens are ideally suited to the muted tones of the Highland landscape.

The artist's palette

Evelyn tends to start her paintings by blocking in the areas of colour and tone with a palette of yellow ochre, raw sienna, light red, cerulean, ultramarine and titanium white. Then, as the painting builds, she adds cadmium lemon or cadmium yellow, alizarin crimson, raw umber, cobalt or Payne's grey and perhaps viridian and magenta. She doesn't often use black.

pointer

Using black

Many artists disdain black, saying it dirties the other colours. It is true that it is difficult to handle and can overwhelm a painting when used neat or heavily in mixes, but a little can be useful for muting other colours. Indeed, Payne's grey, which is often used for this purpose, is actually made from a mix of blue and black pigments, so in effect it is black which has already been mixed. You can mix a very good Payne's grey yourself from ultramarine and ivory black.

lemon yellow

cadmium yellow

yellow ochre

raw sienna

light red

cerulean

ultramarine

cobalt blue

raw umber

alizarin

viridian

Payne's grey

lemon yellow

cobalt blue

cobalt blue

viridian

lemon yellow

ultramarine

Artist's Own Technique

Eveyln can take several months to finish a painting from conception to completion, but in that time she is usually working on several pieces, breaking off from one to start or develop another. Sometimes she may leave a painting for up to a few weeks, partly to allow the paint layers time to dry, but also if she is suddenly inspired by another piece. She works in a traditional way, "blocking in, working from background to foreground, thinned paint first then thicker, then glazes; large brushes to begin with and smaller ones for details; scraping out the bits I don't like, re-drawing areas, painting over other unsuccessful bits until I feel I cannot take it any further."

shortcuts

Tonking

Sir Henry Tonks, Professor of Painting at the Slade School' invented this technique which makes it possible to paint over areas which aren't yet dry. Simply press a piece of absorbent paper on top of the wet area and peel it off to remove excess oil and colour, but be careful if you choose newspaper as the print may come off!

Evelyn does not complete many oil paintings because she works in a variety of different mediums and has recently been working with a combination of paint and print on canvas using acrylic printing inks and acrylic paints.

'I am seldom satisfied with my work but sometimes lucky enough to have bits of my work that I like.'

Eveyln uses large brushes to block in the first stages of the composition and to add texture to the sky.

Thicker, richer paint, applied towards the end of the painting process, helps suggest depth and dimension in areas where fine detail isn't possible, such as this densely wooded area of conifers.

Towards the end of the painting process she also adds details, such as these tree trunks, with smaller brushes.

"My painting is a search for beauty, interpreting Nature and natural forms in a way which asks the viewer to look again and perhaps, with luck, evokes the spirit of a particular place. Because it has been interpreted in paint it becomes in some odd manner a part of the viewer's soul in a way which simply seeing that piece of countryside does not."

"When looking for a landscape I do a lot of driving around. When I see something – sometimes only a glimpse in the rear-view mirror – I stop and walk around. Often I am wrong and the shape I thought I saw isn't there. I feel that if what I'm looking for doesn't 'fire' me, how can I expect it to fire anyone else with the desire to own my version of it? Often, almost in desperation, I have started a painting only to realize that the 'real' painting of that place – the focal point, almost – is not what I am looking at but a little to the right or left."

"I painted this picture at Penshurst. It is a lovely place and I was sure I'd find something to paint. As normal, it took a lot of finding, climbing fences, scrambling down the river bank and trying out the possible angles. I'd seen the house and trees from the road, but it took a lot of tramping around until I could line them up with that bend in the river."

'River Eden, Kent' by Lynette Hemmant oil on board **60 x 40cm.**

Composition

"I painted four pictures of the River Eden from the same field, one landscape-shaped, the one shown here in portrait format, another looking to the left up towards Penshurst Place and the last one looking at the river in the other direction. Sometimes a view is improved by lowering the eye level which means sitting at the easel – I find this more difficult as it is harder to move far enough away to evaluate what one is doing."

golden rule

Curves in composition

Perhaps because few natural objects are dead straight and some, such as the human form can be highly curvaceous, curves in a composition can be very sensual, even animal, and evoke a strong sense of being alive. Straight horizontals can be calm to a point of deadness while strong, straight diagonals and verticals can be so energized that some viewers find them positively overpowering, even offensive. By altering these lines to make them more curved or choosing a view which is curvy already, you can create a composition which takes a middle course and is interesting and lively without losing the relaxed mood we associate with viewing a landscape or being so relaxed that it seems dead.

"I almost never sketch or photograph a scene first. Photographs are always the wrong colours and the perspective is wrong too. I draw if I want a drawing, not for any other purpose unless I am commissioned to do a painting in which case I do a 'bare bones' sort of sketch to show the client how I see it and to assure myself it will work well. I was an illustrator for many years and perhaps I have an ability to see the image in its entirety on my internal screen, and don't therefore need to work it all out first."

'There is a rhythm in landscape; sometimes you see it immediately, sometimes only as you work.'

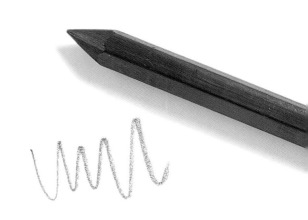

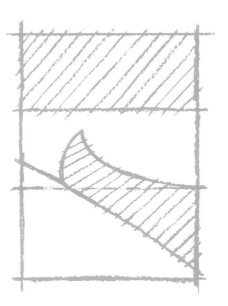

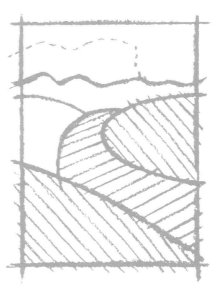

Lynette chose a relatively unusual format for her landscape by turning the board to create a portrait format. The skyline is in the traditional position two-thirds of the way up the picture area, but in this format it gives her a lot more space to develop the landscape and also focuses in on the main subject – the bend in the river.

By choosing to focus on the bend in the river, Lynette makes her painting much more intriguing than if she had painted a straight run of the river. The bend also creates a more relaxed pace than a straight line, swaying us gently along on our visual journey up towards the trees.

Straight lines usually give energy and drama to a painting, but here everything is curved for a gentle sense of movement – if you listen you can almost hear the breeze as it ruffles the trees and plays across the water.

Colour

"I work with natural hues, using mostly earth colours, and I am one of those artists who cannot help but translate what they see into 'real' colour on the board. In spite of the tendency to try, in a painterly way, to represent the scene I see, I also try to enhance some colours so there is a little bit of sparkle. Flake white, used with care, can be very helpful with highlights, and the rather unreal, 'chemical' phthalo blue and green can boost a painting without being vulgar."

The artist's palette

"I use Winsor & Newton artists' colours, sometimes adding titanium white in alkyd form to hasten drying, and I occasionally use a drying medium such as Liquin, though less than I used to. For this painting I used mostly earth colours – siennas, umbers and yellow ochre – with Naples yellow, Hooker's green, phthalo green, Payne's grey, a little red and stronger cadmium yellow. Skies are usually mixed from cerulean and ultramarine for the really blue bits, with all sorts of muddy mixes from the palette to help with the clouds. After all, what's wrong with painting mud with mud?"

'Colour is nothing if it does not accord with the subject and if it does not increase the effect of the painting through the imagination.'

(Eugene Delacroix)

raw sienna

burnt sienna

yellow ochre

raw umber

Naples yellow

cadmium yellow

Hooker's green

phthalo green

Payne's grey

cadmium red

cerulean

ultramarine

phthalo green   yellow ochre

cadmium red   cerulean blue

pointer

Which white?

You could be forgiven for thinking that a white is just a white, until, that is, you go into an art supplier and are confronted by several choices. Luckily there aren't any really bad whites, so you can't go far wrong. Perhaps the best of all is flake white, also called lead white, which is only available as an oil or alkyd. It is strong, warm, opaque, quick-drying and flexible, and you only have to look at an early painting to be convinced of its durability. There are concerns about its toxicity, but provided you don't lick your fingers or chew your nails when painting it should be safe. If you are worried about using flake white, choose titanium (sometimes called opaque white) instead. This is very bright, pure, opaque, totally lightfast and covers well. If you want a transparent white for any reason, choose zinc white which is a cold, inexpensive white. It can crack if applied thickly as an oil, so use it with care.

Artist's Own Technique

"I start by roughing in shapes on my board – more solid than canvas in a wind – using burnt umber or any dirty green paint diluted with turps. If it doesn't work I wipe it off. Once I think the shape is about right I block in fairly simply with transparent colours and then build on it. I do follow the old rule 'fat over lean' in that I start with very diluted colour, feeling my way until I have enough confidence to put it on thick. I work until the light has changed too much – around three hours to start with – then I begin a second painting and maybe a third. The next day the time given to each painting is a little less so that the shadows remain true. I usually manage to complete in four or five sessions, but it depends on the complexity and what I'm expecting from the painting. Rarely do I do a fast, one-sitting painting, and occasionally these come out well, but I'm really one of those people who likes to try to synthesize a place, accepting the small changes from one day to the next, keeping what I like and repainting if I prefer today's sky to yesterday's."

'I enjoy using new brushes but ruin them quite quickly – brushes should be cared for properly, i.e. cleaned and finished in clean water. I would be a big liar if I said I did that every day.'

shortcuts

Painting water

Water, in all its natural forms, is an endlessly fascinating subject, but it is also difficult to capture, particularly when it is moving because it has substance and life yet is transparent or semi-transparent. To capture it well all you can do is observe and keep practising. You will soon see there is a logic and repetition in the way water moves and you can use brushstrokes to describe this. It is imperative not to overwork water, but to stop as soon as you have captured it. Too much paint and too many brushstrokes can make it look solid, like the land.

"There are lots of legitimate 'tricks' in painting but I don't feel comfortable with them. I like wasting time getting the 'treeness' of a particular tree rather than following the usual advice to simplify and reduce."

Notice how details become less distinct in the distance and colours become more muted and bluer in accordance with the rules of perspective.

If you look closely you can see that Lynette has enhanced the colours in some areas with bright green to add the sparkle she spoke of on the previous pages.

Oil 97

LANDSCAPES OILS

"Each of my paintings tells a particular story which I don't verbally need to tell, but which I hope the viewer senses – and perhaps makes a conscious link to some place or someone in their world. When this happens I feel I have succeeded."

"Both these paintings were made when I was still producing a huge body of work about my life amongst the people and wilderness of Eastern Turkey. 'The Settlement' is a painting about displaced people – Kurdish people escaping over the border from Iraq. It is a painting for those people in the tents who the viewer can't see but I remember because I spent a night with one of the families. This painting is for them and it is a painting of hope."

Right **'The Settlement' (1990)** oil on canvas **200 x 220cm** (private collection of Tim Kirkpatrick)
Below **'The Way Home' (1992)** oil on canvas **190 x 220cm** (private collection of Sir Jeremy Isaacs)
by Robert Maclaurin

"On one of my walkabouts in an area of Far Eastern Turkey, I met a young shepherd. I spent two days and nights with him and his flock and his big white dog which hid among the sheep, protecting them from the threat of wolves. We would hear them howling at night in these isolated high pastures. 'The Way Home' is about this shepherd. It is a portrait of him in 'his' landscape where he spent all his life. So it is a painting for him of his well-worn journey that he treads many times a year."

photographs of paintings by Hyjdla Kosaniuk

'My paintings are very personal responses, often relating to a specific person, place or chain of events in my world.'

Composition

Trained in the Scottish Art School tradition, Robert has a good founding in drawing and composition, but for him the motivation or experience which triggers a painting and the way he responds to it is also of major importance if he is to produce a convincing work. "I am always drawing in sketchbooks but this might not be used for a painting at all. I am just as likely to make a major work from a description of a place in a journal – I call it 'a written sketch' – and it is very important that I record these emotions and feelings at the time of making small drawings and vague colour notes. I have to hold on to these thoughts in order for a painting to be made with conviction."

The high viewpoint, looking down on the village in the valley below, not only creates a wonderful sense of space, but allies us with the unseen shepherd who watches the village while overseeing his flock and it shows how far he has travelled from home. Despite the distance of the village, the white line of the road which leads the shepherd home is clearly defined and draws us in.

"Like the other painting, 'The Way Home' was the result of very small sketchy ink drawings done in a sketchbook at the time. What really is more important and why these drawings eventually produced a canvas of 190 x 220cm was the experience."

golden rule

High viewpoints

Most landscapes are painted pretty much straight on which helps to create a sense of being there, but choosing a different viewpoint, from above or below, say, can produce a very striking image. Looking down on somewhere from above can convey the excitement of seeing a place for the first time after a long journey, like looking into a new world. It can also provide a sense of seeing without being seen.

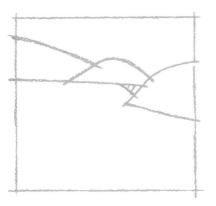

The cluster of Kurdish tents is placed towards the middle of the composition, showing that the people have come a long way, but still have a distance to travel. They can also be seen as representing all people on the journey of life. Their size – each tent is barely as big as a small tree – shows how small Man is in the context of Nature.

The softly shaped hills in the foreground and middle distance suggest that the people are moving to a better place, away from the harsher region represented by the barren, jagged hills in the distance.

"Constructed out of a week's walking through Kurdistan in 1988, 'The Settlement' is a transient picture. I used three drawings that I had made that week and turned them into one to make this large oil on canvas back in my studio in Edinburgh two years later. I don't like to analyse too much, but the tents are halfway in the painting under a softer set of hills than the harsh, pointed, inhospitable ones the people have travelled from. Like the people with their tents, the painting is a journey in itself; layers of paint painted over layers of earlier paint."

Colour

"I have often used paint colour as an emotional element in my work: these paintings are depicted not how I saw them but how I remember the experiences that eventually led to the individual paintings."

Robert uses the near-complementaries orange and green ('The Way Home') and muted complementaries greyed blue and soft orange ('The Settlement') to add intensity to the images, showing the strength of emotion aroused. The colour combination in 'The Settlement' is generally more peaceful than that in 'The Way Home', perhaps suggesting that the Kurds have overcome the worst and can move forward with confidence and hope. The strong colours in 'The Way Home' may suggest the adrenaline rush of keeping watch over the flock while the wolves howl all around.

The artist's palette

"I have always used the best quality paint. I never compromise on this, and the same goes for my stretchers and canvas: I use only the best. My paintings are my voice, so it is in my interest that they last for many centuries; quality materials and sound techniques will allow my voice to survive through my paintings. I use artists' quality Schmincke and Winsor & Newton oil paint."

cadmium yellow

yellow ochre

cadmium red

cobalt blue

oxide of chromium

burnt sienna

burnt umber

permanent alizarin crimson

cadmium yellow

cadmium red

cobalt blue

oxide of chromium

cadmium yellow

yellow ochre

pointer

Mixing your own greens

Choosing a ready-made green is a difficult matter. Many, such as sap, olive and terra verte are not always lightfast, so most artists choose viridian or chromium oxide green. Viridian is lightfast with wonderful transparency, while chromium oxide is an opaque, dull, mid green, also very lightfast. Both are strong and can stain colours laid on top, so they require careful handling. Because of this many artists choose to avoid ready-made greens altogether and mix their own from yellows and blues. This is most satisfactory, since it is easy to mix wonderfully subtle tones in this way. Robert Maclaurin often mixes his own greens.

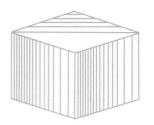   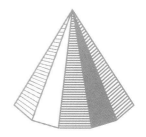

Artist's Own Technique

Robert paints in the traditions of his Scottish Art School training, with a strong sense and bold use of colour and good discipline in drawing and composition. But the real lesson was learned later, "when I had to teach myself the discipline of working a six-day week in the studio and develop a great belief in myself as a painter".

"At the time I was working in quite an impasto way with paint, building up layers of paint over the top of other layers of dried paint. I have a mental picture of what I think the painting will look like but it never turns out that way. For example, I have a rough idea that I want an expanse of trees, but each individual tree is never carefully planned, I like the idea that these large pictures form themselves by a journeying process very similar to the way the subject matter forms the basis for the paintings in the first place."

The journeying subject matter of these pictures at the time was completed when the paintings had finished their own physical journey of being painted. As a painter I feel as if I'm always half in control of something very wild that will eventually be tamed. It never gets easier."

Capturing tone

In the words of Paul Cézanne (1839–1906)' the progenitor of Cubism; "all forms in Nature adhere to the cone, sphere and cylinder" and this is useful to keep in mind when considering how the tones should vary across an object. Capturing tone is quite complicated and deserves proper study, but basically if an object is lit from one side the lightest part does not necessarily face the light directly and the darkest part face furthest away. Instead both the lightest and darkest areas will tend to face the onlooker slightly (see diagrams above). A certain amount of reflected light bounces back from the surroundings, lighting the very edge of the darker side.

'The joy and difficulty of painting is getting the original inspiration to form into something strong and beautiful.'

shortcuts

Impasto

This technique takes its name from the Italian word 'pasta', meaning paste and it refers to the method of applying paint thickly so that the marks of the knife or brush are evident in the finished work. Each artist's idea of what constitutes impasto is different. For some it means applying paint straight from the tube and layering it on the canvas in thick peaks. To others it means simply applying paint thicker than normal so that it is only slightly diluted, perhaps with oil but not turps, and to Robert it means applying many layers of paint to build up texture. Since very thickly applied paint can crack as it dries it is best to put it on in thinner layers or to mix the paint with impasto paste or fast-drying alkyd medium to reduce the chances of cracking. This also makes the paint go farther.

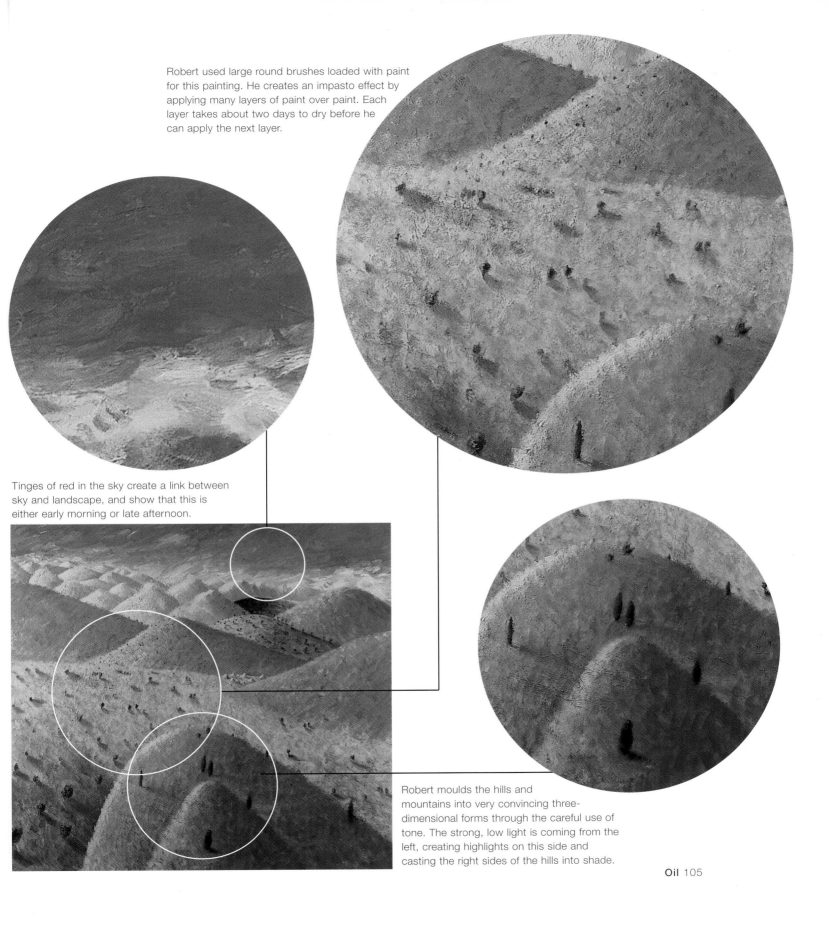

Robert used large round brushes loaded with paint for this painting. He creates an impasto effect by applying many layers of paint over paint. Each layer takes about two days to dry before he can apply the next layer.

Tinges of red in the sky create a link between sky and landscape, and show that this is either early morning or late afternoon.

Robert moulds the hills and mountains into very convincing three-dimensional forms through the careful use of tone. The strong, low light is coming from the left, creating highlights on this side and casting the right sides of the hills into shade.

MIXED MEDIA

LANDSCAPES MIXED MEDIA

Neil Canning's work is bright, vibrant and overflowing with the thrill of Nature. He is interested in Man's effect on the landscape "through mining, farming and worship" and this is important in determining the atmosphere he tries convey in his work. For him, as for many artists, the experience of being in the landscape is a vital part of his work, and he needs to get to know an area before he can begin to paint it: "I tend to spend many hours walking and experiencing a landscape before images develop from it. For me, light, weather and geology are equally important elements in defining the basic landscape."

'Burning Summer' by Neil Canning mixed media on paper **56 x 76cm.**

Composition

At the centre of Neil's work is the vitality of Nature – the living, moving, changing landscape which is beneath our feet. A certain knowledge of the history of a particular place helps him tap into this barely seen but often perceived force. "What is happening – or has happened – beneath the surface helps to convey a much stronger feeling of how the land is composed. Study of ancient stones or bronze age walls hints at the mystery of what has gone before."

Many of the forms of Nature are universal – the slope of a hill, the form of a tree, "circles in stones, field patterns or natural curves and lines," and Neil uses this to good effect in his compositions. As he says, this repetition, when translated on to paper or canvas "helps to unify the various elements of the composition whilst creating natural movement and rhythms." You can certainly see similarities of form between these two paintings, their sweeping, curving lines reflecting the energy and power of Nature and the almost frightening intensity which Neil puts into his work.

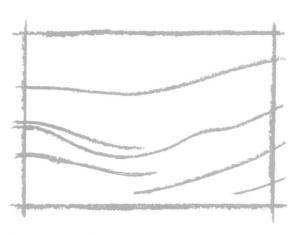

'Burning Summer' has the more relaxed composition of the two paintings, though still energized and intense. The long, sweeping curves that swoop from left to right and from right to left create a rocking, breathing movement, almost as if we are watching waves rolling at sea.

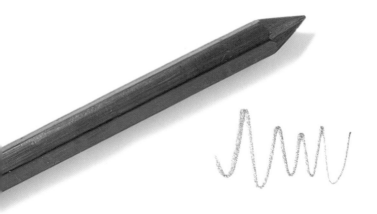

'Splintered Earth' by Neil Canning
mixed media on paper **81 x 102cm.**

In 'Splintered Earth' the thicker, more aggressive sweeps of colour create a much more angry or dynamic feel as if the earth really is rising up and splintering in front of our eyes with the intensity of a volcano.

Streaks of black and white cut through the painting like lightning bolts, filling the image with power so you can almost hear it fizzle and spark.

golden rule

Curves and straight lines

In general, compositions based around curves keep the eye moving at a leisurely, rhythmic pace, retaining the viewer's interest, yet creating a fairly peaceful mood. They can be sensual too, as if the viewer is visually stroking an animal or even the human form. Straight, horizontal lines are dead calm, but tilt them and they become suddenly energized – in general, the steeper the slope, the more energy in the line and the greater the sense of speed. In 'Splintered Earth' lines travel from top left to bottom right, creating a rapid sense of movement and intense energy.

Because the lines of colour are straighter and more direct than those in 'Burning Summer' they create movement of a much faster pace.

Colour

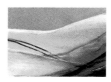

Obviously Neil's colours do not reflect the actual colours of a place. Instead they are designed to convey his response to it. He chooses strong, vibrant colours – cerulean or rich ultramarine, viridian and cadmium yellow – and places them next to each other so they really sing. Unusually, he also sometimes uses pure black, but he doesn't use it for mixes; instead he applies it straight on to the paper, creating rich, dark areas which make the other colours seem even richer by comparison and almost edible, they are so luscious.

The artist's palette

Neil uses a range of paints: Unison or Sennelier pastels; Daler Rowney designers' gouache or watercolour and Rembrandt oils. This takes advantage of the different qualities of each type – the purity and intensity of pastels, the clarity of watercolour or gouache and the rich depth of oils. He always chooses colours with high lightfast values to ensure durability.

pointer

Using pure colours

Neil uses very bright, pure colours which other artists might find too hot to handle. Place them in a figurative landscape and they might well jar, but used together they feed off each other to sizzle like electricity. Even colours which most other artists eschew, such as black, behave well when balanced by equally powerful hues. Indeed, the black acts like leading in a stained-glass window, absorbing light so none of it bounces into the neighbouring colours, leaving them pure and intense.

cadmium yellow

cerulean blue

ultramarine

viridian

yellow ochre

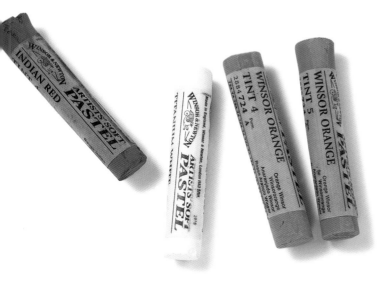

All colours convey their own moods, and their personal associations mean that each person responds differently. As Emil Nolde (1867–1956) said, "yellow can express happiness, and then again, pain". But whatever associations you may have with the colours Neil uses, they are bound to be fairly intense. This is because they are so strong – muted colours are far more tranquil than brilliant, pure hues.

'Every colour harbours its own soul, delighting or disgusting or stimulating to me.'

(Emil Nolde)

palette knife

Artist's Own Technique

Neil aims to interpret the life force of Nature in his paintings: "light may dissolve form into shimmering shapes and wild brushstrokes gash the colour beneath to suggest fierce cross-winds." He also recognizes the softer face of Nature and notes that "the primitive, wild beauty of the land is always balanced with the gentlest of touches, hinting perhaps at dew or sunbleached grasses."

He paints on 300g Cold Pressed Arches watercolour paper or linen and applies paint with brushes and knives in a free, expressionistic style.

'My wish to communicate the sheer thrill of being outside often means that I employ strong colours and strong rhythmic gestures.'

shortcuts

Using painting knives

There are two basic types of artist's knife: the palette knife and the painting knife. Palette knives have stiff blades and are designed for mixing paint on the palette. Painting knives are more flexible and are used to apply paint to canvas, board or paper. They come in various shapes to produce different marks. They can seem more difficult to use than brushes, but many artists enjoy the sensation of using them to apply paint and they make it possible to apply anything from the merest scraping of paint to thick, textured layers.

painting knife

The painting process is even more vigorous in 'Splintered Earth' than in 'Burning Summer'. Notice the way that black paint is allowed to flare up into the blue sky, like dust flying up from a volcanic eruption. Paint strokes are long and sweeping, and in some areas, such as the white in the foreground, the paint even seems to have been splattered on.

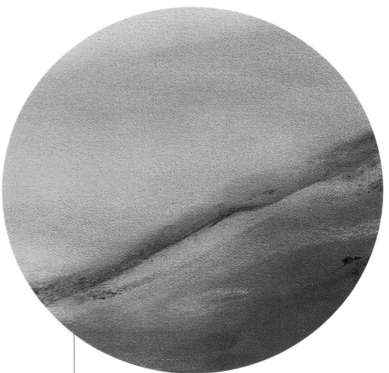

Consecutive washes of colour help to sculpt the landscape and hint at the softer face of Nature. Smudges of pastel have a further softening effect.

A strong wash of gouache creates a bright, solid mass of colour for the sky.

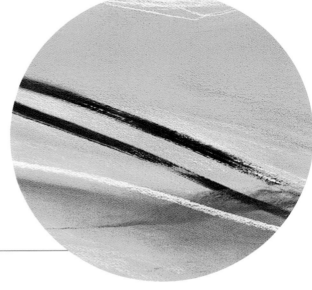

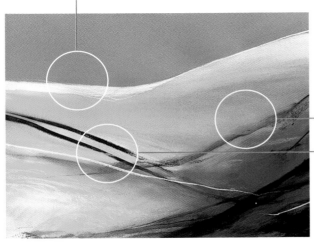

Streaks of black gouache and white pastel, applied at the end of the painting process, add dynamism and provide added textural interest.

"The starting point for each of my landscapes is a photograph either one taken by me during my travels or one found elsewhere, in books, magazines, calendars etc... I respond to those landscapes whose unique qualities of texture, pattern, translucency and opacity, for example, can readily be conveyed by a range of media of analogous qualities."

"I found this particular image in a book about Spain. Its appeal to me was the way space is defined not through traditional perspective but by the stacking up of planes of colour and texture from the bottom to the top. You see this effect exaggerated in the finished painting to emphasize the surface texture."

"When I first started painting my main inspiration came from pre-Renaissance and non-European art forms: Pompeiian frescoes, for instance, or folk art from around the world; those arts, in other words, which emphasize simplicity and surface decoration. Not surprisingly, it is the work of Henri Matisse that appeals to me – he embraced those very influences. More recently the American Edward Hopper, with his deceptively modest aim to 'simply paint sunlight on the side of a house' taught me the importance of light and shade in the creation of relief on a flat surface, and its role in the suggestion of mood."

'Spanish Landscape with a Row of Trees' by Lydia Bauman mixed media on MDF panel **122 x 122cm.**

'My inspiration comes from those arts which emphasize simplicity and surface decoration.'

Composition

"I use the square format rather than the more customary horizontal rectangle because it is easier to organize spatially and because it compels the viewer to perceive the painting not solely as a scene but as an object in its own right. I deliberately eliminate as much of the sky as possible in order to give emphasis to the much more textured land and so draw attention to the surface of the painting."

"It is only the foreground trees, with their volumes clearly defined by light and shade, that give a sense of three dimensions to what would otherwise have been a completely flat painting. It is this dialogue between the reality of the three-dimensional world and the reality of the two-dimensional picture that is the true subject of this and all my other paintings."

golden rule

Pre-Renaissance styles

Before the middle of the 15th century when painters started to become fascinated with perspective, artists were more concerned with motifs and their meanings and with creating an image which was decorative and pleasing. Grace and harmony were produced by the artist's intuitive placement of the features rather than by conforming to a mathematical plan. Lydia's work has much in common with this early style of art – her work is attractive in its own right and not just as a copy of a scene in Nature.

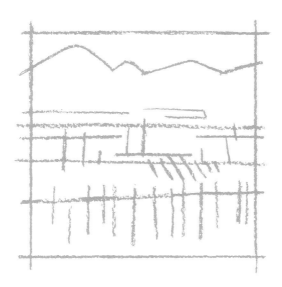

Lydia often selects landscapes with high viewpoints or images of hillsides which have very little sky so that she can devote as much of the painting as possible to developing the textures of the land.

The scene is viewed as a series of horizontal planes. Although the distant mountains are bluer than the foreground and middle-ground areas in accordance with the rules of perspective, this has more to do with the colours in the original image than any attempt to push back the hills into the distance. At all times Lydia wants us to be aware that this is a painting, not a real scene.

Colour

"Green is the least favourite colour for me – very inconvenient for a landscape painter! In my experience green has to be just right, otherwise it looks quite wrong, but getting the colour right or 'lifelike' is the least of my preoccupations. Rather, I like to take liberties with colour, preferring it to make sense instead as part of the aesthetic whole of the painting."

"I invariably use pigments which are soluble in water because of the demands of my technique – powder paints for mixing with wax, or acrylics, gouache or watercolour for mixing with plaster. My favourite range comprises some pure pigments (some less pure than others) which I brought back from a market in India a few years ago. They are very intense in colour and live in cheap little plastic jars which I also procured in India."

The artist's palette

Because Lydia makes her own paints, it would be impossible to list what she uses. She utilizes a whole range of colours added to sculptors' wax, resin or other mediums and sometimes introduces materials from decorators' suppliers such as bitumen and tins of pretend granite etc. (see next pages).

Lydia may not like green but she manages to create some stunning variations of it in this painting. Notice how the bright, vibrant greens in the foreground constantly pull the eye, as does the violet blue of the distant hills, so our eyes constantly bounce back and forth between them.

Using pigments

Pure pigments can be purchased from specialist art shops and used to create all sorts of different paints. A traditional medium is egg tempera, which is made by adding fresh egg yolk – the fresher the better – to ground pigments. Since there is no known solvent for egg, this creates one of the most long-lasting paints of all. It was used in Medieval pieces, such as the Wilton diptych, whose stunning colours testify to its durability. Other mediums can be added to pigments too – gum arabic to make watercolour, linseed oil for oil paint or even melted beeswax. You can even add pigments to plaster as Lydia does.

'I like to take liberties with colour.'

Artist's Own Technique

"I paint entirely in the studio, never in front of the motif, using the snapshot as an aide-memoir and the starting point for a rigorous process of simplification and reordering of the composition. If I am lucky the photograph I have taken or have found might already be a 'Bauman', with no need for major alterations, but this is rare, and besides, it is the reordering and simplifying that is such a gratifying part of the process."

"The media I use rarely come from art shops, though these do have a very useful range of texture gels. I go to Do It Yourself shops to get bags of Polyfilla into which I mix my pigments to spread on my MDF panels fresco-style. I also add tins of roofing bitumen, tins of pretend granite and other finishes used in decorating. Suppliers of sculpting materials provide the resin I use for other interesting textures, as well as different types of wax, which, with its ability to both absorb and reflect light, is so good at conveying the subtleties found in landscape."

"Last, but not least, sand brought back from travels to different corners of the world makes an appearance in the paintings of these places, though it always amazes me how different it ends up looking on a panel in a studio in the East End of London than it looks in its own setting. Also extraordinary is how different in colour and texture sand can be from places such as Cuba, Jamaica, Spain or the Negev desert."

shortcuts

Creating textures

There are all sorts of ways of creating attractive textures in a painting, particularly when using mixed media. Lydia gives her paint more body with plaster (Polyfilla), wax and gel, as well as artists' texture mediums. Other ways of adding texture include using acrylic modelling paste. The thickened paint can be applied with a spatula or brush and then left as it is or combed with a glue spreader, steel comb or home-made card comb cut to shape. Impressions can also be made with crumpled foil or even bubble wrapping, a coin or other tool.

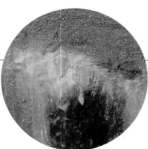

Lydia used a sharp instrument, such as the end of a paintbrush to scratch definition into the trees and shrubs of the middle distance. This is a technique known as 'sgraffito'.

Using ordinary, fairly cheap, basic brushes, Lydia dabs texture into the foreground tree canopies. The process of painting in this way is both expressive and satisfying.

Mostly Lydia uses a plastic spatula to apply her materials but to create added texture, as in the foreground earth, she uses the serrated edge of a glue spreader; the sort provided free with certain adhesives.

LANDSCAPES MIXED MEDIA

Andie Clay's vibrant and exciting landscapes are drawn from life, memory and the imagination. Like the paintings shown here, they are often based on sketches of the moody, historic region of North Pembrokeshire, West Wales, near Andie's home. They are developed in her studio to reflect the soul of the place and her emotional responses to being there.

'Carn, Storm Brewing' depicts Garn Fawr, an Iron Age fort which rises steeply from the coastline "often described as a dragon's crested back". This distinctive landscape is part of the ancient volcanic eruptions which formed the land. Andie has been to the place often and feels the importance of its origins. "It was this feeling of something restless and simmering under the Earth's crust that I wanted to convey – almost as if it could erupt again. I aimed to express my feelings about the almost frightening power of Nature, of its ever-changing contrasts, harmonies and discords. To visit a place such as this on a balmy summer's day is but one aspect – to visit it in mid-winter with gale-force winds and horizontal rain attacking from every direction begins to make you appreciate such power."

'Carn, Storm Brewing' by Andie Clay mixed media on paper **72 x 90cm.**

Composition

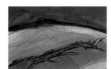

"Using Nature's patterns and forms as a starting point, I wanted to convey a feeling of being on top of the world, of endless blue sky and land receding into the distance, so I experimented with the use of an elevated viewing point to create the feeling of floating above the Earth's surface. I both accentuated and simplified the curves of the hills to form a background that balanced the strengthened curve of the Earth's crust, while using the 'cap' of forestry on the right to add height to the overall composition. The strong diagonal of the track leads the eye into the painting and contrasts strongly with the network of sheep trods [paths] shown as abstract floating patterning. I deliberately made no attempt to 'ground' these."

'Golden Road' by Andie Clay mixed media on paper **72 x 90cm.**

golden rule

Using paths or tracks

Some artists prefer their landscapes without the mark of human habitation – overhead cables, fences, parked cars and roads – sometimes even editing out buildings, although cultivated land is usually considered acceptably rural. However, these things can have great impact and meaning in a painting. As well as showing Man's presence – for good or ill – they can have huge use compositionally, helping to lead the eye deeper into the painting, as in 'Golden Road'; or 'fencing it in' at the edges and preventing the eyes from wandering away from the main focuses of attention.

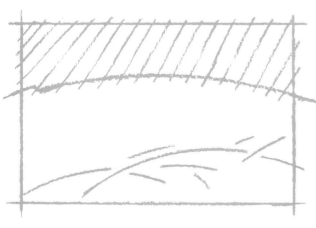

To lead the eye up to the line of curving earth Andie placed the foreground rift diagonally "which makes the eye zigzag quite strongly". She used strong, dark tones in the top third of the painting to help hold the eye within the picture area.

"To help create the feeling of immense power and restlessness under the Earth's surface I experimented with the positioning of the carn, choosing to offset it at an angle and accentuate the sweep of the Earth's crust. The stormy sky helps emphasize the mood I sought to create and allows the carn to stand strongly in the top third of the painting."

'Although I attempt to be a human sponge and continually absorb and get my inspiration from Nature, I make no attempt to be a camera or to record the colours as seen.'

Colour

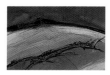

Andie has a wide collection of different media, all in large colour ranges, but she rarely uses colours straight from the tube or jar, preferring to mix her own. She thinks carefully about colour and often uses black – not in her mixes, because it can turn them to 'mud', but as a foil for bright colours, often overlaying pastels on top of an area of black ink to enrich them as in 'Golden Road'.

"My colour palette varies according to the mood and feel I am attempting to convey. The expressive use of colour allows me total freedom to work from memory, imagination and experience. The one colour that rarely appears in my landscape painting is green."

"In 'Carn, Storm Brewing' I used analogous colours in both the sky and on the land, the purples and yellows acting as complements but balancing each other because of the proportions used – 1/3:2/3. In the sky I used mainly red-purple pastels; on the land I used reds, yellows and oranges, with reds, purples and blues on the carn itself."

cadmium yellow

cadmium orange

cadmium red

ultramarine

cerulean blue

burnt sienna

The artist's palette

Andie uses a vast array of colours, brands and media. Among them are pastels by Rowney, Rembrandt, Sennelier and Unison; Acrylic inks by FW and Magic Colour; acrylic paints by Liquitex, Rowney, Winsor & Newton and Golden paints; gouache by Winsor & Newton; and St Petersburg Artists Watercolours which come in whole pans, large enough to fit her brushes.

'My work has to be about what I feel, first and foremost.'

"In 'Golden Road' I also chose an analogous colour scheme, with turquoise blue/purple being the dominant colours, hoping to create a feeling of space and distance. I experimented with overlaying closely related green-blues and red-purples and blue-purples to add depth and interest. I largely ignored the use of aerial perspective [colours getting weaker and bluer the further away they are]; distant tones are lighter, but not less pure, as is usually the case. The yellow of the road was echoed on the distant horizon with flashes of golden yellow pastel defining the change from land to sky."

pointer

Analogous colours

Quite simply, analogous colours are those that appear next to each other on the colour wheel – yellow and orange, blue and violet and so on. In practice you can mix a wide range of analogous colours yourself from two adjacent primaries. If, for example, you mix a warm yellow such as cadmium yellow with a warm red such as cadmium red in various proportions you'll obtain a range of harmonious analogous yellows, oranges and reds. The same applies if you mix a primary with an adjacent secondary, although the range of colours created will be narrower.

cadmium yellow   cadmium red

'My work seeks to convey the earth's rhythms and energy flows and to convey a sense of the spirit of the place.'

Artist's Own Technique

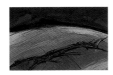

"To me it is essential to get to know a place before I attempt to paint it. Regular visits allow me to experience its many moods and to develop my feelings for it. This is vitally important as it feeds back into my expressive approach to my work."

"I use a location sketchbook for visual notes made on site and sometimes I also sit and draw for the sheer joy of it. I work on thick watercolour paper which does not need to be stretched so I can work fast and use sheet after sheet. I always tend to work in series and produce a range of paintings about a location. This may result in only one painting that I am happy with, but the process of experimentation has been of prime importance to me and cannot be cut short."

"Working on the floor with my board at a slight angle, I mark out the basic skeleton, usually with black ink. My favourite drawing instrument is the pipette that comes in the FW acrylic ink bottles; it makes endlessly fascinating and varied marks and there is a long flow of ink. Other instruments used regularly are goose quills, stencil brushes, fan blenders and old-fashioned Post Office nibs which give a beautiful and varied width of line depending on the pressure applied." After this, Andie goes on to apply liquid colour before switching to an upright studio easel so she can apply the pastel colours easily. Sometimes she leaves paintings out of sight so she can come back to them afresh – this happens at every stage, even once she thinks it is finished. This is because Andie likes to, "keep my work alive at all stages and to remain open to chance up to the last minute".

shortcuts

Mark-making
This is one of the most exciting means of expression available to the artist using drawing tools. Both students and experienced artists can learn much from sessions devoted to exploring the range of marks possible with specific tools, such as charcoal, pastel sticks, pen, biro, quill and so on by applying them upright, on their sides, dragging them backwards, forwards and sideways, pressing hard or lightly. These newly discovered marks can then be used in a picture to express a subject's texture, its weight or character as well as the artist's mood and the emotion he or she wishes to evoke.

Post Office nib

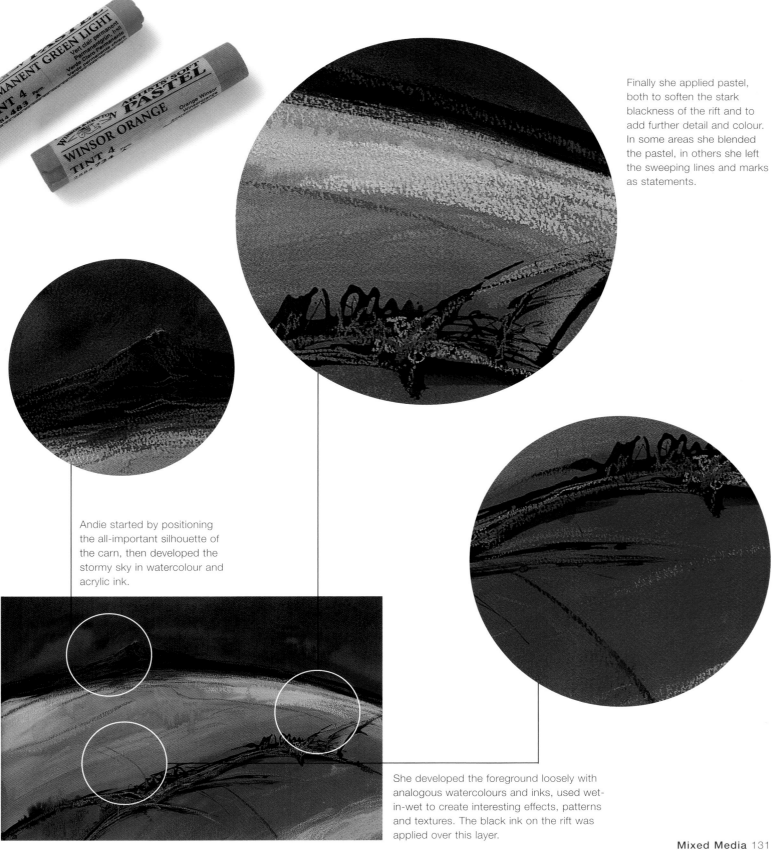

Finally she applied pastel, both to soften the stark blackness of the rift and to add further detail and colour. In some areas she blended the pastel, in others she left the sweeping lines and marks as statements.

Andie started by positioning the all-important silhouette of the carn, then developed the stormy sky in watercolour and acrylic ink.

She developed the foreground loosely with analogous watercolours and inks, used wet-in-wet to create interesting effects, patterns and textures. The black ink on the rift was applied over this layer.

acrylic

LANDSCAPES ACRYLIC

Frank Bentley is an entirely self-taught artist who didn't start painting until he was in his early 40s after working as an electrician and antique-shop dealer. He is normally placed amongst the naive school of British painters and paints from the mind, "rediscovering that state of happiness and innocent well-being that childhood memories usually hold for us". His paintings are drawn neither from life, nor entirely from the conscious imagination, but based on scribbles from his unconscious mind.

'Four Spotted Cows'
acrylic on board
61 x 61cm.

'Three Fields, Four Horses'
acrylic on board
56 x 61cm.

'The Lake'
acrylic on board
66 x 63.5cm.

'Six Spotted Cows in a Field'
acrylic on board
61 x 61cm.

by Frank Bentley

Composition

"My compositions for landscapes are drawn from nothing more than lines on paper. Quite often they consist of a jumble of scribbled lines drawn with a black biro on A4 paper. They are scribbled down without looking or with my eyes closed. What I am doing here is creating a source for inspiration to make a picture. Just as we stare at the clouds in the sky and see or imagine the shapes of animals and people, so I, too, will stare at my jumble of lines and look for a landscape. By using some lines as contours of hills and others as boundaries of fields, lakes or ponds, I compose a picture."

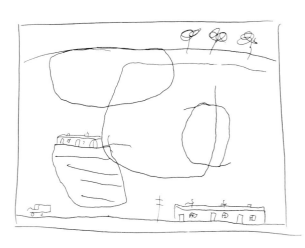

golden rule

Naive painting

Naive painting, also known as primitivism, is characterised by the use of bright colours, child-like perspectives and unpretentious subject matter. Artists of this school ignore the current trends in art and stand outside the conventions. One of the most famous naive painters is Henri Rousseau (1844–1910) whose enchanting jungle paintings were much admired by the Cubists, among others.

"At this stage the composition in the top sketch has no right or wrong way up – I rotate the scribbled drawings and view them from all four sides of the paper as I stare at and into the maze of lines, seeking out some hidden composition that would make an interesting picture. It doesn't always work, of course, and lots of scribbled drawings finish up in the bin, but it is fun to do and exciting when I discover a possible new landscape hiding amongst the scribbles."

Frank has taken this original scribbled sketch and adjusted and developed it to create the finished composition (far left). Notice that most of the fundamental elements of the finished painting are present in the sketch.

If Frank can see a landscape in one of his scribbled drawings he develops it further, either elaborating it directly or transferring the main contours on to another sheet of paper to develop there. Notice how similar this painting is in composition to the original sketch.

All Frank's compositions start out as scribbles in black pen, drawn with his eyes closed or without looking.

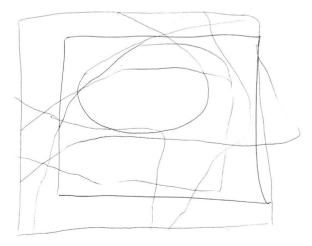

Colour

Frank sometimes uses colours appropriate to the scene, as in 'The Lake', but not always, feeling free to use colours from his imagination that seem to fit in with his personal style. "I don't always use the appropriate colours for a particular scene. I'll try something different, as in 'Three Fields, Four Horses'."

The artist's palette

Frank uses a limited colour palette of permanent yellow, crimson, ultramarine, cerulean (coeruleum), deep violet, titanium white and Payne's grey or black, "preferring to mix other colours, like green, on the support or palette, rather than buy them ready-made". He tends to use Daler Rowney Flow Formula Acrylics.

'Because my pictures are created, in the main, from my imagination, I feel I can take liberties with my use of colour.'

permanent yellow

alizarin crimson

ultramarine

cerulean blue

deep violet

Payne's grey

Mars black

permanent yellow   cerulean

permanent yellow   ultramarine

alizarin crimson   cerulean

About blue

Ultramarine was one of the first blues. Made from the semi-precious stone lapis lazuli, it was so expensive that only rich clients, such as the Church, could afford it. It came to be associated with the Virgin Mary and was often chosen for her garments. Perhaps because of its value, artists often left it pure, unmixed with other colours. Today artists have many wonderful blues at their disposal, including the gorgeous opaque green-blue cerulean; phthalocyanine blue which is also greenish and intense, but transparent; and cobalt, a good mid-blue. Modern ultramarine, made artificially, is the only true violet blue and therefore hugely popular with artists.

pointer

Mixing clear colours

Mixing colours isn't as easy as we are led to believe at school. If you mix any blue with any yellow, for example, you may not get anything like the green you require. For a good, clear green seek out a greenish yellow, such as lemon yellow, and a greenish blue, such as cerulean. That way you will produce a very green hue. Likewise, to produce a clean violet, mix a violet red, such as quinacridone violet with a violet blue, such as ultramarine, and so on. If you simply can't mix the colour you want, it may be you need to invest in a new ready-made colour.

Artist's Own Technique

Frank paints on either canvas or MDF board. He starts with a charcoal or pencil drawing and then develops it with paint, sometimes leaving the underdrawing exposed as part of the finished painting "so a finished painting often resembles a painted drawing".

Frank has a special technique of mixing his paints with decorators' filler. "Here lies a story as to why this little trick of mine came into being. Because I'm so impatient for quick results – and paint rather quickly as well – I chose acrylics for their quick-drying ability. However, what I didn't like about acrylics was their plastic-looking finish, even if matt varnish is used. I much preferred the matt, chalk-like finish that oil paints produced, but unfortunately oils are so slow to dry. So I experimented and found that by mixing decorators' repair filler with acrylics, I obtained a near-exact matt finish to that of oil paints, plus the filler added texture and body to the acrylic paints, which I also liked."

"The downside to this mixture is that it chokes up brushes very quickly, so they have a short life. Because of this I use very cheap round hog-hair brushes for the main areas and small squirrel-hair brushes for the details. I also have a tendency to use them like scrubbing brushes which doesn't help their upkeep!"

shortcuts

Charcoal and acrylic

Charcoal and acrylic is a wonderful combination. To allow both to shine through in a painting, as in Frank's work, artists tend to use paint thinly, like watercolour or gouache. The charcoal lines can also be redrawn at the end of the painting process – or part way through – to strengthen them and redefine any areas that need it.

Frank starts with a pencil or charcoal underdrawing which is often allowed to show through in the final painting.

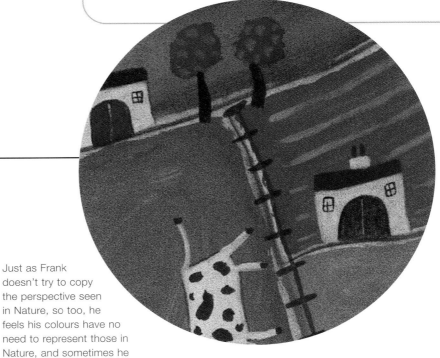

Alkyd paints

Frank invented his own medium to achieve the texture and drying time he required, but new paints are being produced all the time which may be just what you want. For artists in a hurry, the new alkyd paints offer an interesting alternative to oils. They handle in the same way as oils but are dry in a day or two. They can be mixed with oil paints in which case they speed up the drying times of the oils and can be used on surfaces primed for oil or acrylic paint. They are also useful for underpaintings – oils can be reserved for the top layers of paint, speeding up processing time considerably.

By mixing decorators' filler with his paints he achieves a matt, chalk-like finish, similar to that of oils.

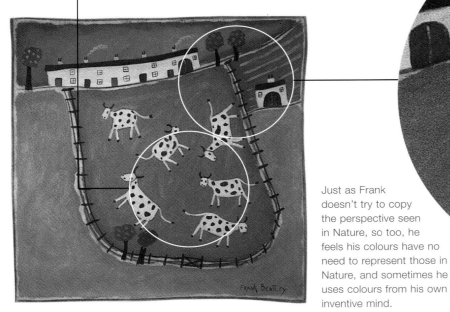

Just as Frank doesn't try to copy the perspective seen in Nature, so too, he feels his colours have no need to represent those in Nature, and sometimes he uses colours from his own inventive mind.

With its blue sky, fresh green field and ancient red-roofed buildings, this tranquil scene captures all the romance of Italy. It is as if we have just chanced upon the houses while on a country walk, perhaps searching for a picnic spot or a quiet place to read.

However, for David Evans it was not the picturesque nature of the scene that caught his eye but its colours and shapes. "I was inspired to paint this particular scene in the mountainous area of Tuscany by the way the light caught the pinks and yellows on the buildings. The tall trees, by contrast, gave a certain amount of excitement to the otherwise placid and peaceful scene before me."

'Tuscany Landscape' by David Evans acrylic on board **25.5 x 20cm.**

Composition

David was struck by the negative shapes in the trees which created a sense of movement and depth – he knew this would make a good painting. He was also drawn by the contrast between the trees' hard strong shapes and buildings and the relaxed, uncomplicated area of the foreground field. "The basic composition was inspired by the way the foreground shapes contrasted vividly with the pattern of angular shapes created by the buildings." To create a balance between these two distinct areas, David gives more space to the 'light' field and sky than to the 'heavy' buildings and trees.

The obvious composition here might have been to place the buildings in the centre of the support, just as you would in a snapshot, particularly as there is very little to focus on in the foreground field. However, David's composition is much more successful, creating as it does a sense of movement and of exploration. By squeezing the buildings into the top-left corner of the support, he leaves us peering at the painting, wanting to see round the corner, as it were, to glimpse more of the view.

Placing the busy buildings and trees in one corner like this also helps create a tranquil image by giving the majority of the picture area over to the simpler greenery and sky. However, not all artists could attempt this – it relies on the fact that David is so expert at rendering the subtle shapes and colour differences between the wild plants and flowers in the field.

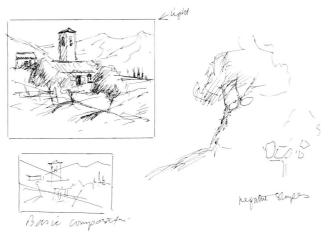

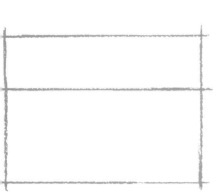

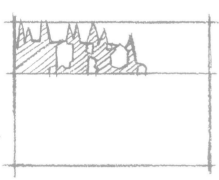

David places the horizon roughly two-fifths of the way down the picture area rather than in the more popular position one-third of the way down, and he squeezes most of the 'activity' into just one-fifth of the painting. This leaves us curious and wanting to see more.

Whereas the foreground field contains very subtle contrasts, the sun reflecting off the walls of the buildings and casting deep shadows from the trees creates much stronger contrasts. This gives the buildings and trees a much denser, 'heavier' feel.

By limiting the proportion of the picture given over to the buildings and trees David creates a well-balanced image with a restful mood. The busy, 'heavy' activity of the buildings is counterbalanced by the soothing, 'light' areas of field and sky.

golden rule

Negative shapes

Negative shapes are probably something only artists think about. They are the shapes around and between objects – the curved space between a jug handle and the jug, for example, the spaces between the spokes on a wheel or between a tree in a painting and the edge of the support. Artists find it helpful to look at these spaces when trying to paint a subject accurately. So, for example, instead of painting a tree trunk and its branches, they draw the spaces between the twigs, trunk and branches, leaving a silhouette of the tree remaining. This is a particularly helpful exercise when learning to draw.

Pen & aquarelle pencil   Church of St. Stephen on Lake Garda

Colour

David uses a fairly compact basic palette which has everything he needs to render most subjects. However, like most artists he might introduce new colours for a particular series of paintings or omit some. He might also introduce just a dab of a certain colour where it's needed in a particular picture.

The artist's palette

"For this series of paintings I mainly used buff titanium, red iron oxide, raw sienna, Naples yellow, cadmium yellow pale, cadmium red, cobalt blue, French ultramarine, Payne's grey and titanium white."

buff titanium

raw sienna

cadmium red

red iron oxide

cobalt blue

French ultramarine

Payne's grey

cadmium yellow pale

Naples yellow

red iron oxide   raw sienna

cobalt blue   Naples yellow

cadmium yellow pale   ultramarine

pointer

About iron oxide

A number of the warm, rusty browns come from synthetic or artificially produced iron oxides. These colours are similar to the earth colour burnt sienna, but are usually less transparent and some are redder or pinker. The Mars colours, such as Mars red or Mars brown are included in this group, along with Indian red, Venetian red and red oxide. All these colours are reliable with good lightfastness.

7003 146 No.21

Artist's Own Technique

"I prepare my board or canvas with a thin wash of buff titanium and when dry I start blocking in my basic shapes. For linear marks I use the edge of a plastic card and for broader shapes a rolled-up kitchen towel as I like to move my composition around the support."

"Next I build up my shapes of colour with a painting knife, allowing my acrylic paint to become a little more sticky before applying it to the painting." As David develops the painting he often mixes in matt glaze medium to create lovely translucent glazes that enable him to build up a rich depth of colour. He sometimes heightens colours to produce special effects such as that of reflected light.

'The great way to paint with acrylics is the very old-fashioned method of glazing with washes.'
(David Hockney b. 1937)

shortcuts

Painting with found objects

Using tools other than brushes or knives to paint with gives an image a whole new facet by introducing new shapes and textures. Often along the way it also produces lively marks which, sometimes quite by accident, perfectly create the shape that is required. David uses the edge of a piece of plastic to make strong, sharp linear marks, but artists can experiment with all sorts of things. The cap from a tube of paint could be exactly right for capturing the fruits in a tree, for example, or the corner of a plastic sandwich wrapper might render the shape of a bird in flight.

David uses the edge of a piece of plastic to create linear marks – to render the corner of a building or the shadow under the eves, for example.

By allowing the paint to dry a little and become sticky before applying it to the support, David is able to create lovely rich textures.

By vigorously smearing closely related greens in the foreground with the painting knife David ensures that the field is lively enough to retain our interest yet still maintains its tranquil effect.

pastel

LANDSCAPES PASTEL

"I have lived in North Wales all my life and find so much about the landscape that is inspiring that I never produce paintings anywhere else – there is enough on my own doorstep to keep me occupied. A good forecast is often the only inspiration I need. Reasonable weather for me means anything apart from rain, although really strong winds can be a little off-putting – diffused, watery light is so much a feature of Welsh meteorological life that we come to expect it."

"Maps are another source of inspiration – the evocative place names, the reminders of past expeditions and conquests. Memories are aroused of the perfect picture missed because the cloud descended, or the sun refused to come out and the vow to return again when the conditions and the time would be right. The back-burner of my mind is full of so many slumbering thoughts of many distant, enigmatic hills and farmsteads, that the mere smell of an Ordinance Survey map will breathe life into them once more and rekindle the burning desire to paint."

Top **'Moelwyn Sky'** pastel on board **43 x 58cm.**
Centre **'Llyn Brenig'** pastel on board **46 x 61cm.**
Bottom **'Druids' Circle'** pastel on board **41 x 56cm.**
by Alwyn Dempster Jones

'The mere smell of an Ordinance Survey map will rekindle the burning desire to paint.'

Composition

golden rule

Diagonal divisions

Diagonals give energy and impact to a painting, creating a generally more dramatic effect than horizontals – notice how calm and timeless 'Druids' Circle' seems compared with 'Moelwyn Sky' which is much more energized. Diagonals also suggest movement – we know that an object on a tilted surface is likely to move whereas on a flat base it will stay stationary. In 'Moelwyn Sky' we know that the landscape can't move, so the sense of movement is subconsciously transferred to the clouds.

"I had spent a long autumn day wandering in the mountains that rise spectacularly and dominate the slate community of Blaenau Ffestiniog, and had been engrossed in a number of detailed studies of lichen-covered slate, when there was a little movement in the late afternoon air, with a clear sky apart from the odd clump of slowly moving pink-lined clouds. The dipping sun had produced a dark mass of featureless mountain but had added colour and subtlety to the clouds."

Intrigued by this particular viewpoint, Alwyn set about capturing it. "I dissected the paper from left to right, slicing the picture in two unequal parts to create tension. The cloud was the most important element, so it dominated the composition; the slope of the line would imply movement in the cloud. The mountain will always be there – you can see it on a map and it doesn't move, but that cloud has disappeared for ever."

"High above the sea, nestling on a wind-blown stretch of moorland and looking out across the Irish Sea and the mass of Great Orme's Head, stands Meini Hirion or Druids' Circle. My mother had often talked about the place and the weather forecast was good, so I had high hopes, but what I encountered was a dull, damp day with intermittent watery sun and an impenetrable cloud base at about 800ft. The stone circle covered a much larger area than I had expected and offered little compositional inspiration. I was not happy. The next two profitless hours were spent crouching at ground level and exploring loftier vantage points to try to get this pile of old rocks into something like a picture. I gave up, turned and walked away – I had been wasting my time. As I descended I took one final glance. The stones presented themselves in silhouette with their stark shapes puncturing the late-winter sky. The effect was magical. Here at last was a painting."

"I now found myself focusing beyond the stones and into the strong, bright light of the setting sun. By concentrating on the sky, the original object of my attention had been stripped down to dark, simple shapes that grew out of the dark brown earth. The wind had dropped as it so often does at the end of the day, and the stones were silent, still and alone. The approach to the painting was now relatively straightforward. As time slowly ebbed away I made shorthand notes about the mood I wanted to create together with sketches of the stones in silhouette and a number of small but detailed cloud studies."

Colour

The colours of a Welsh sky, with the possible exception of a dramatic sunset, tend to be soft and subtle. Alwyn does not seek to exaggerate these, but keeps his colours soft, muted and realistic. As you can see from his colour notes on the margins of his sketches (previous page), his colour selection for these skies is very limited, ensuring an overall harmony.

Mixing colours

Pastel stands out from most artists' mediums because you can't mix a colour you require from others, though you can overlay hues so that, to an extent, they mix in the eye. This means that you need to buy many more pastels in a range of tones and shades in order to create the effects you want. In other mediums, for example, you don't need to buy grey as a good range can be mixed from other colours, notably by mixing complementaries (see page 63), but when painting landscapes in pastels you may find you need quite a selection.

"With bright, clear light Llyn Brenig looks for all the world like a jagged piece of mirror that has fallen from the sky and come to rest on a bed of dark heather. The distant reflections in this mirror are a series of precise lines etched in a brilliant white or darkest grey whilst the foreground is one of a subtle gradation from light to dark grey."

The artist's palette

Most pastel artists have a huge range of colours, too subtly different to name. Alwyn is no different, but he tends to use pastel pencils which come in much more limited ranges than soft pastels. "Encased in wood and with numbered barrels, they can be sharpened to a point to give a greater degree of detail and precision."

For these pictures Alwyn used pastel pencils from two different ranges (Conté and Schwan Stabilo Carb Othello), although the subjects only required a small number of colours. In general he uses three brands: Conté pencils, which he likes for their softness, making them good for blending; Schwan Stabilo Carb Othello which are his personal favourites because they are "excellent for fine detail" (especially brown No 635 and green No 585 which is "ideal for Welsh grass"); and Rexel Derwent, especially 'chocolate'. He also uses Rotring art pens with a fine nib and black ink or an extra-fine nib and sepia ink.

For 'Moelwyn Sky' Alwyn knew he would "need an instrument that was infinitely cruder and less refined than my usual pastel to render the razor-sharp edge of the mountain that cut into the ice-blue sky, so I reached for pen and ink." On top of this he used pastels to create the subtle effects of the sunset, with the warm, fading light reflecting off the underside of the clouds and kissing the peaks of the landscape.

Artist's Own Technique

Alwyn usually makes sketches on site with detailed studies as back-up, perhaps focusing on cloud forms, stones or rocks. Back in his studio he sets about making the final painting. He always works on conservation-quality board with little surface texture which allows him to paint directly onto it without the need for stretching, and the relative smoothness allows him to blend and merge colours.

When painting 'Llyn Brenig' Alwyn started with the shape of the lake since this is a constant and the foundation of the whole work. He applied a light watercolour wash to the area surrounding the lake to give weight to the lower part of the painting.

For 'Druids' Circle' he used a watercolour underpainting for the foreground, before adding layer upon layer of pastel. As he darkened the foreground the light in the sky seemed to become brighter through contrast. "The key to the success of the painting was the contrast between the light amorphous sky together with its implied movement and the solid, immovable stones which have stood for centuries."

Right and below
By deepening the colour in some areas and leaving the merest trace in others, Alwyn creates extreme contrasts which add to the drama and substance of his skies.

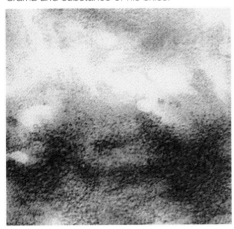

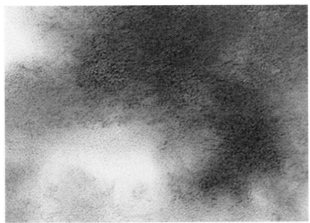

Above: Alwyn used pen and ink to render the sharp line of the mountain's edge which cuts the painting in two.

Left: By softly blending the pastel marks, Alwyn is able to capture the light, amorphous nature of clouds in a way which is nearly impossible in any other medium.

shortcuts

Using pastel pencils

The success or failure of pastel pencils as a medium can be put down to how they are handled. If pressed hard they will etch into the paper, leaving deep trails which are difficult to blend and erase, though this will add texture, which some artists like. By using the pastels lightly, however, you will be more in control and can build up colour depth gradually and subtly. Move the pencil round, using the tip for defining lines and the side for lighter shading and blending.

"This painting came out of my head as one of a series of imaginary landscapes/cloudscapes using some new pastels I had purchased from Unison in Northumberland, but the inspiration came from my experience of skies in the North East of England." The other elements of the composition grew out of Lionel's emotional and visual response to a particular landscape and from his interaction with the pastel pigments. "The idea for the track running across some tidal mud flats came straight from my experiences walking across Morecombe Bay at Cartmel Sands. The atmosphere of light and colour came from the way the pastels flowed on to the paper and my intuitive engagement with the process of applying and removing these rich pigments."

'Track' by Lionel Playford pastel on paper **37 x 63cm.**

'In this imaginative landscape emotion was everything and really the painting spoke to me as it evolved.'

Composition

"This painting owes its composition to a dialogue with other paintings of my own and with other painters, in particular William Turner and Ivon Hitchensand, plus, to some extent to American and British abstract expressionist painters of the '50s and '60s. Another important aspect of the composition was its rhythm and its symmetries. There is a rhythm in the shape and placement of patches of colour which owes as much to the internal logic of the painting as it does to the appearance of real clouds and real mud flats. This can be compared with musical composition. I suppose this painting, and others like it, are like musical improvisations with some basic structure such as the horizon more or less fixed at the start of the composition and some concept of feeling and shape held at the back of one's mind during the creation of the piece."

Lionel chose a very short, wide format, like a photographer's panoramic picture. This emphasizes the immensity of the view and conveys a tremendous sense of space. Try cropping off part of the image and you'll see how important this wide format is for the painting's effectiveness.

golden rule

Foreshortening

The modern mastery of perspective can be put down to one man, an Italian architect called Filippo Brunelleschi (1377–1446) who gave artists the mathematical means of solving the problem of foreshortening (things looking smaller as they get further away from us). From then on artists had the means of producing effects of startling realism. One major component of correct perspective is the use of a vanishing point. You can see this at work in Lionel's painting – the parallel lines of the track converge as they retreat towards the vanishing point on the horizon.

The horizon line is plotted just one-fifth of the way up the picture area. This, combined with the sheer width of the painting, helps to create the impression of being on a wide-open plain.

Through a skilled use of foreshortening Lionel gives depth as well as breadth to the painting – see how the clouds get closer together as they recede, as do the lines of the track.

'During the time of making this picture my entire perceptual experience of skies, tidal mud flats and the making of drawings and paintings were brought to play on one rectangle of paper.'

Colour

It can be tempting with pastels to amass a huge collection and try to use all your favourites in a picture, letting colour run wild. If you're not careful this can result in a cacophony of clashing or conflicting colours. Lionel has a way of avoiding this. "I deliberately limited myself to a range of browns, pinks, blues and greys which were picked out of my large selection of pastels before the painting was started. This was to ensure some degree of control over colour." He worked on an orange-yellow paper which influenced his choice of colours, this has a unifying effect and sets the tone for the painting.

Lionel always likes to use Unison pastels which he says are "greatly superior to many other makes I have tried for a number of reasons. The pigments have subtle and interesting variations. The sticks have a useful flat cigar shape and all vary slightly in size and shape because they are handmade. I like knowing that a craftsperson made them – there is a great deal of love in those sticks. They are fairly strong while at the same time the pigment flows off the stick smoothly and generously."

'There is a great deal of love in those sticks.'

pointer

Optical colour mixing

Pastel is an ideal medium for trying out the Pointillist technique of optical colour mixing. This technique is based on the idea that instead of mixing red and warm yellow to make orange, for example, you place tiny amounts of red and yellow next to each other on the picture so that from a distance they blend to make orange – but a more lively orange than using orange pigment would achieve. Georges Seurat (1859–91), who devised the technique, used dots of colour, but the effect works just as well in tiny strokes or cross-hatches.

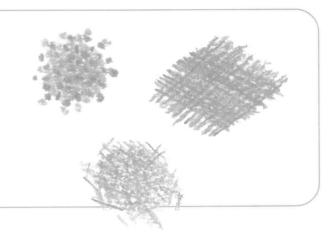

Artist's Own Technique

"I work by simply applying the pigments one on top of the other, often using the broad side of the pastel and then smudging, blending and erasing pigment back through the layers, sometimes down to the base colour of the paper." This process is repeated in many areas so the final composition is "merely the trace left behind after this long intuitive process of change." Lionel compares this with processes in Nature – particularly apt given his subject matter. "It seems to me that this is similar to what goes on in cloud formations and in the tidal estuary as the flood tide wipes the slate clean twice a day."

'As far as tools are concerned I use whatever comes to hand which includes fingers (different ones for different colours), cotton rags, French sticks, plastic erasers and cotton wool.'

Sometimes Lionel erases colour back down to the base colour of the paper using cotton rags, a plastic eraser or cotton wool.

shortcuts

Using fixative

Many artists don't approve of using fixative, but some find it easier to control the loose texture of soft pastel by fixing the picture at regular intervals – a system comparable to building up an oil painting. Spray the fixative lightly to keep colours clean and prevent smudging. Fix the finished picture in the same way. For artists who prefer not to use fixative, the finished picture can be pressed under a sheet of tissue to embed the colour more firmly in the paper grain. Mounting the picture behind glass will also offer protection.

The tooth of pastel paper can quickly become clogged with colour, so Lionel starts with loose, light marks, covering all areas of the picture to develop it at the same rate. This is the best way of producing a balanced result.

Lionel builds up the colours, overlaying pastel strokes and blending the various hues by smudging with his hand, fingers or a rag.

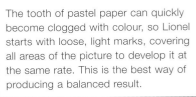

Portfolio

'Hoo Hole'

'The River's Source'

'The River's Broken Course'

Fish in the Old Mill Dam

'Burning Summer'

'Clearing Storm'

'Splintered Earth'

'Spanish landscape with trees'

'Spanish landscape with a row of trees'

LYDIA BAUMAN was born in Warsaw, moved as a child to Israel and then on to England where she completed a BA in Fine Art at the University of Newcastle followed by an MA in History of Art at the Courtauld Institute of Art, London. She has since worked professionally as a painter and freelance art history lecturer, primarily at the National Gallery. She has exhibited her work extensively and her paintings can be found in collections around the world. United Airlines, Warner Bros., and Saatchi and Saatchi are among the corporate collectors of her pieces. Her work can be seen at: Rebecca Hossack Gallery, 35 Windmill Street, London W1P 1HH (tel: 0171 436 4899); at Catto Gallery, 100 Heath Street, London NW3 1DP (tel: 0171 435 6660); or at her home, 24 St Mark's Rise, London E8 2NL.

FRANK BENTLEY is a self-taught artist working in the naive style who lives and works in West Yorkshire. His work has been exhibited in many galleries including The Mall Galleries, London; The Manchester City Art Gallery; Leeds City Art Gallery; The British Work House Gallery, Dallas, Texas, USA; and Andre & Rosamon Jane Mas, Naive Art Collection Exhibition, Monaco. His work is also held in The Galerie Eisenmann, Aichtal, Germany. He can be contacted at his studio: 8 Church Bank, Cragg Vale, Hebden Bridge, West Yorkshire HX7 5TF (tel: 01422 886 760).

PHILIP BRAHAM is a Scottish painter who trained at the Duncan of Jordanstone College of Art in Dundee and the Royal Academy of Fine Art in The Hague, Holland. He has won numerous awards for his work and participated in many solo and group exhibitions. He now lives and works in Edinburgh. His work can be seen at: Boukamel Contemporary Art, 9 Cork Street, London W1X 1PD (tel: 0171 734 6444; fax: 0171 287 1740).

NEIL CANNING studied in the studio of a professional artist. He held his first one-man exhibition in 1979 and since then has held many more. His work has been shown at many prestigious galleries and exhibition halls including the Royal Academy, London and the Paris Salon, and features in many public and private collections throughout Europe, America and the Far East. Recent sales to collections include A.T. & T.; Ford Motor Co.; Kleinwort Benson Investment Management; Mitsubishi Corp.; SmithKline Beecham and many more. His work can be seen at: The Old Post Office, Farmers, Llanwrda, Dyfed, Wales SA19 8LQ (tel: 01558 650 743).

'Mountainscape'

'Mountain Gullies'

ANDIE CLAY studied at the London College of Printing and has a BA Hons degree in Graphic Design. She has participated in many exhibitions around Britain and won numerous awards. She lives and works in North Wales and can be contacted at her studio: Porth, Blaenporth, Cardigan, Ceredigion, North Wales, SA43 2AP. (Tel/fax: 01239 810 713; web site: http://stdavids.co.uk/artspace /andie.htm.) Galleries which regularly exhibit her work include the Tabernacle. The Museum of Modern Art, Machynlleth; The Albany Gallery, Cardiff; and The Attic Gallery, Swansea.

'First Growth'

'Harvest Home'

STEPHEN COURT is predominantly a landscape painter whose concerns "are about ways of looking, seeing, showing and sharing". He studied at Yeovil School of Art and Birmingham College of Art & Design and won a Royal Academy David Murray Travelling Scholarship. He not only paints himself but has taught painting, drawing, print and graphics. His work can be seen at: Lupton Square Gallery, 1–2 Lupton Square, Honley, Huddersfield HD7 2AD; The Loggia Gallery, 15 Buckingham Gate, London SW1E 6LB; Tidal Wave Gallery 3 Bridge Street, Hereford HR4 9BW; and the Cupola Gallery, 178A Middlewood Road, Hillsborough, Sheffied S6 1TD.

'Wall'

'Farm near Dogellau'

ALWYN DEMPSTER JONES studied at the Flintshire School of Art, Manchester College of Art & Design and University College, Cardiff. His work has been exhibited widely in Wales and the rest of the UK and his paintings are held in public and private collections both in Britain and abroad. His work has also appeared in numerous publications. He can be contacted at: Cedryn, 24 Ffordd Trem y Foel' Parc Bryn Coch, Mold, Flintshire, North Wales CH7 1NG (tel: 01352 704 084 or 01352 756 017).

'Still Life with Fish'

'Siena'

KATY ELLIS graduated from The Glasgow School of Art in 1995 and in the same year won the Royal Scottish Academy's John Kinross Scholarship for painting in Florence. The following year she won the Stoke-Roberts Painters and Stainers Travel Award and also the Winsor & Newton Young Artists Award for Watercolours. She travelled and painted extensively during 1996 and 1997 in Italy. Her work can be seen at: The Burford Gallery, High Street, Burford OX18 4QA, England.

'Venice Reflections'

'Lone Fisherman'

DAVID EVANS studied at Llanelli, Swansea College of Art and served in the Royal Marines, travelling extensively. The main source of inspiration for his paintings comes from landscapes, here and abroad and he is particularly interested in the effects of ever-changing light. He has participated in numerous exhibitions in London, Bristol, Cardiff and New York, amongst other places, and his work is held in many collections, both private and corporate including the House of Lords, London, the National Library of Wales, Beckenried, Switzerland and Hotel Pleiadi, Tuscany, Italy. To see more of his work, contact him at his studio: 24 The Crescent, Burry Port, Carms, Wales SA16 0PP.

'Strelitzia'

'Lobster'

'Brooke Cottage, Kent'

'Cottages, Somerset'

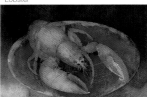

'Landsong 37'

'Rochas 9'

'First Light, Purnululu'

'In the Silent Land'

SHIRLEY FELTS graduated from the University of Texas in 1960. She has travelled widely, sketching and painting in Japan, Nepal, America and South America. Her work is in public and private collections in Britain and abroad. She has illustrated books for adults and children and in 1995 won the Conservation Book award for 'The Blue Whale'. In 1996 and 1997 she worked as Artist in Residence for the Iwokrama Rainforest Research Programme in Guyana. She painted aspects of the forest from the field station on the Essiquito River. One of these paintings was presented, in 1996, to the late President of Guyana, Dr Chedd Jagan. Her work can be seen at:
Alex Gerrard Fine Art,
Bell Lodge, Vinehall,
East Sussex TN32 5JN.

LYNETTE HEMMANT was brought up in South Wales, Australia and England. She studied at St Martin's School of Art, London and then worked for many years as an illustrator. She has taken on a number of interesting art jobs including designing a set of stamps for the island of Guernsey and illustration work for the prestigious American children's magazine 'Cricket', but her first paintings were sold by the Bolzani Gallery, Milan in 1985. She has homes in Italy and England and her painting mainly concentrates on landscapes and gardens there, both real and imaginary. Contact her at:
35 Camberwell Grove,
London SE5 8JA
(tel: 0171 703 6186).

THIRZA KOTZEN studied at the University of the Witwatersrand, Johannesburg, South Africa; the Central School of Art and Design, London, England; and the University of Oregon, Oregon, USA. She has won numerous awards and honours and has considerable teaching experience. Impressively she has held eleven one-person exhibitions, many at the Curwen gallery in London but also in Johannesburg, and has participated in many group exhibitions around the world. Her pieces are held in private collections and by a range of institutions including IBM, Paris; Bank of China, London; and Anglo American, South Africa. Her work can be seen at: The Curwen Gallery,
4 Windmill Street,
London W1P 1HF
(tel: 0171 636 1459).

ROBERT MACLAURIN is a Scottish artist based in Edinburgh, Scotland. He trained at Edinburgh College of Art and after graduating won a Turkish Government Scholarship to paint in Istanbul. His paintings are in many private and public collections including The Contemporary Art Society and The Scottish National Gallery of Modern Art. In 1995–96 he worked in the Dunmoochin studio in Australia on a Sir Robert Menzies Fellowship and in 1998 he won the Noble Grossart Scottish painting prize. His work can be seen at: Berkeley Square Gallery, London (tel: 0171 493 7939)

'Country Path'

'The End of Summer'

'Invermoriston'

'Signs of Spring'

'Irises, Loch Auchenreoch'

'Track'

'The Bridge in Autumn'

'Renands Farm, Sault Vancluse'

'Brittany Landscape'

HUGH MCNEIL MCINTYRE studied at Rhode Island School of Design, USA and Edinburgh College of Art. He has travelled widely to paint in numerous countries including Germany, France, Italy, Spain and Brazil. His paintings are held in numerous prestigious collections including those of HRH The Prince of Wales and The British Linen Bank Headquarters, Edinburgh; The Robert Flemming Collection; PDC, New York; Ashai Optical Co. Ltd. Tokyo; Brunell University and more. His work can be seen at:
The Contemporary Fine Art Gallery, 31 High Street, Eton, Windsor, Berkshire SL4 1HL (tel: 01753 854 315; fax: 01753 620 390).

LIONEL PLAYFORD studied naval architecture and worked in shipbuilding before taking courses in fine art at Cumbria College of Art & Design, Newcastle Polytechnic and then Newcastle University where he gained a BA degree. He is currectly studying for a Masters degree in the subject. He has participated in many exhibitions in London, Newcastle, Edinburgh, Florida, Ohio and Ireland. His work can be seen at:
New Academy Gallery, Windmill Street, London (tel: 0171 323 4700); Moreton Street Gallery, 40 Moreton Street, London (tel: 0171 834 7773); and Chandler Gallery, Hunton, Bedale, North Yorkshire (tel: 01677 540 403).

EVELYN POTTIE is a painter and printmaker who exhibits regularly in many venues in Scotland where she lives and works. She gained her formal art training at Grays School of Art in Aberdeen and now works part-time as a print-making technician for Highland Printmakers Workshop & Gallery, now called art tm, based in Inverness. She completes a limited number of paintings each year, and prefers to work in a print-making medium, usually screenprint or a mix of print and acrylic paint. Her subject is the landscape and she spends a lot of time drawing outside and researching the history of the area. Contact her at:
Art studio tm, Inchmore Hall, Kirkhill, Inverness (tel: 01463 831 798; email: evelyn@pottie.demon.co.uk).

SALLIANN PUTMAN studied at the West Surrey College of Art & Design where she gained a BA Honours degree in fine art. She is an associate member of the Royal Watercolour Society. Her studio is in Berkshire, but she also paints in many areas of Great Britain, in France and in Venice, working in oil, watercolour or mixed media. She exhibits in various galleries in South East England and in a number of galleries in the United States. Her work can be seen at:
Bankside Gallery, 48 Hopton Street, London SE1 9JH (tel: 0171 928 7521) which is the home of the Royal Watercolour Society.

ANDREW WALKER lives in Scotland and gained a BA Hons degree in Drawing & Painting from Edinburgh College of Art. He has held numerous solo exhibitions, both in Scotland and England and has participated in many group exhibitions throughout the UK. His work is held in private and public collections in Scotland and abroad. His work can be seen at:
The Firth Gallery, 35 William Street, Edinburgh. (tel: 0131 225 2196); and Cyril Gerber Fine Art, 148 West Regent Street, Glasgow (tel: 0141 221 3095). Alternatively contact Andrew at Wasps Studios, 3 West Park Place, Dalry Road, Edinburgh (tel: 0131 313 2484).

Glossary of Colours

Here is a brief guide to the different qualities of paint colours used by the artists in this book. Note that paints vary from brand to brand and from medium to medium so always check with the manufacturer's descriptions of the paints. For best results use a good brand of artists' quality paints such as those by Winsor & Newton.

alizarin crimson – popular violet-red; transparent; oil colour can crack if it is applied thickly; watercolour is prone to fading when applied thinly; not totally lightfast

brilliant green – bright, light green; opaque; fairly lightfast

brown madder alizarin – similar in colour to burnt sienna; fairly transparent; low tinting strength; may fade; stains overlaid paints

burnt sienna – clear earth colour made by heating raw sienna; similar to Indian red; transparent when very diluted, opaque with less dilution; absolutely lightfast

burnt umber – made by roasting raw umber; transparent when very diluted, opaque with less dilution; absolutely lightfast; fairly powerful tinting strength

cadmium lemon – the lightest, coldest yellow; greenish; very lightfast; quite strong tinting power

cadmium orange – intense bright orange; opaque; lightfast; fairly powerful tinting strength

cadmium orange deep – similar to cadmium orange in quality but a deeper colour

cadmium red – bright, warm red; opaque; totally lightfast; good tinting strength

cadmium red deep – similar to cadmium red in quality but a deeper colour

cadmium yellow light – bright, cool, pale yellow; opaque; very lightfast, though as a watercolour it can fade in bright, damp conditions; quite strong tinting power

cadmium yellow medium – clean, warm yellow; opaque; very lightfast though as a watercolour it can fade in bright, damp conditions; quite strong

cadmium yellow – clean and bright; opaque; lightfast; reliable

cerulean blue – bright greenish blue; opaque; tends to granulate in watercolour; lightfast; quite low tinting strength

Chinese white – type of zinc white but with greater covering power used in watercolour; cold; bright

cobalt blue – originally derived from crystals; transparent; lightfast; weak tinting strength

deep violet – generally opaque; lightfast; rather weak tinting strength

flake white – derived from lead and therefore highly toxic if taken internally, even in small doses, so don't paint and eat your sandwiches at the same time; wonderfully bright white; only suitable as an oil or alkyd; used by the Ancient Egyptians and Chinese; extremely durable

flesh tint – creamy pink; opaque to semi-opaque; lightfast

Indian red – originally derived from red earth; economical brown-red; absolutely lightfast; covers well

indigo – deep, inky blue originally derived from plant leaves; may be fugitive

light red – earth colour; generally opaque; absolutely lightfast

magenta – bright violet-red; lightfastness varies from brand to brand

Mars black – deep, dense black; opaque; lightfast; very strong tinting colour

Mars brown – warm, reddish brown very similar in colour to burnt sienna originally derived from iron oxide; opaque; absolutely lightfast

Mars red – originally derived from iron oxide; generally opaque; absolutely lightfast; good mixer

Naples yellow – usually a delicious blend of cadmium yellow and white; opaque; lightfast

oxide of chromium – colour varies slightly according to brand; opaque or semi-opaque; lightfast; quite powerful tinting strength; reliable

Payne's grey – soft blue-black; lightfastness depends on the brand; covers well

permanent alizarin crimson – violet-red; transparent to semi-transparent; moderately lightfast

permanent yellow – fairly bright yellow; despite its name, not all brands are lightfast so check pigment content

phthalo blue – intense blue; transparent; lightfast; strong staining colour

phthalo green – vibrant blue-green; highly transparent; lightfast; very strong tinting and staining power

Prussian blue – deep greenish blue; transparent; very powerful tinting strength; lightfast, though some brands bronze with age; similar in colour to the reliable phthalo blue

purple madder – rich red-wine colour; transparent; permanent

raw sienna – soft yellow earth colour; good opacity; absolutely lightfast

raw umber – warm brown earth colour; cool, greenish brown; can darken over time; lightfast

red oxide – derived from synthetic or artificial iron oxide; similar in colour to Indian and Mars red; colours vary according to brand; semi-opaque; good lightfastness

rose madder – originally derived from the madder plant; wonderful soft rose colour; transparent; some brands are extremely fugitive so check with the manufacturer's details before you buy

sap green – originally produced from buckthorn berries; soft, earthy green; lightfastness varies according to brand but may only be moderate

sepia – originally derived from the ink sac of cuttlefish or squid; dark, black-brown;

lightfastness varies according to brand

sky blue – intense cool blue; transparent; lightfast; strong tinting power

terre verte – green earth pigment used since early times; fairly opaque; lightfastness depends on the brand; low tinting strength

titanium white – inexpensive bright white; not as toxic as flake white; very opaque; absolutely lightfast

ultramarine – originally derived from lapis lazuli and therefore highly prized; wonderful bright violet-blue; transparent; absolutely lightfast; good tinting strength

vermilion – a bright, intense orange-red, similar to cadmium red; moderately lightfast as a watercolour

viridian – excellent, strong, clear bluish green; lightfast; transparent; stains overlaid colours readily

Winsor red – rich red colour; transparent to semi-transparent; lightfast

yellow ochre – muted yellow earth colour; generally strong; similar to raw sienna but more transparent; absolutely lightfast

zinc white – cool white; more transparent than other whites; lightfast; dries hard

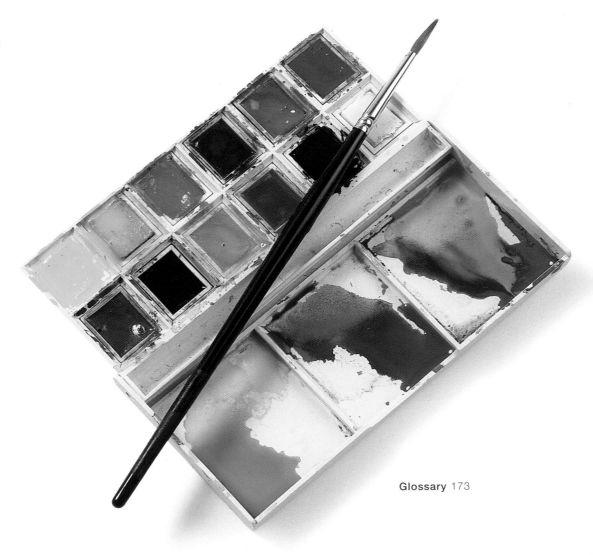

Glossary of Terms

Acrylic – a fast-drying, modern painting medium made by combining pigment with acrylate resin. It handles like oil paint or alkyd when thick and like watercolour when thinned, and it dries quickly to a water-resistant finish which does not yellow. Acrylics are water-soluble when wet so they are often adopted by painters who work in mixed media. Liquid acrylics have the quality, feel and colour depth of ink.

Alkyd – a modern type of oil paint that dries much quicker than oil. It may be used on its own or combined with oil paint to speed the drying time.

Binder – the substance which binds the pigment together to make paint such as gum Arabic or linseed oil.

Blending – the method of combining two colours where they meet so that it is impossible to tell where one colour ends and the next one begins. Blending is usually done with a brush, rag or finger.

Broken colour – where colours are applied next to each other in small amounts so that from a distance they appear to mix. The result is a shimmering effect which captures the qualities of light very well.

Complementary colours – opposites on the colour wheel. Examples are red and green; yellow and violet; blue and orange. When placed together complementary colours seem to make each other look more vibrant, but when mixed they create soft neutrals. Compare with split complementaries.

Drybrushing – the method of skimming a small amount of undiluted paint over the surface of the support to leave a broken trail of colour.

Earth colours – pigments derived originally from coloured earth. These include terre verte, a soft green, and yellow ochre, sienna, umber and Indian red which range in colour from soft yellow to brown.

Egg tempera – a traditional paint made by mixing fresh raw egg yolk with pigment and oil. The paint dries within seconds of touching the paper so it suits artists with a meticulous approach. Today ready-made tempera is available, although most artists who use the medium still prefer to make their own. This is perhaps the most durable of painting mediums.

Fat over lean – refers to the traditional technique of starting an oil painting with paint that has been thinned with turpentine or another thinner, then progressing to pure paint or paint mixed with oil for the final layers. This means that the first layers dry quickly and corrections are easy to make, while the top layers take longer. It also helps to prevent cracking which can occur when thinned paint is applied on top of oil-rich paint. The technique can also be used with alkyds or acrylics.

Fugitive – a paint which fades over time or through exposure to light.

Glaze – paint applied in a transparent or semi-transparent layer to modify the colour underneath. A glaze can intensify or dull down the colour beneath it.

Golden Section – the division of a support along geometrical lines to create the 'perfect' proportions (see the Introduction). The rule of thirds is a similar, simpler method of positioning the main features.

Gouache – an opaque water-based paint which is handled much like watercolour. It is particularly popular with illustrators and graphic designers because of its bright colours and matt finish. Adding plenty of water to the paint makes it more like watercolour, but used neat it has good covering power and unlike watercolour it can be applied to coloured grounds.

Ground – a prepared painting surface such as a primed canvas. The primer can be tinted in which case the surface is called a 'coloured ground'.

Gum arabic – the medium used in watercolour to bind the pigment. Additional gum arabic can be added to make the paint more transparent and glossy. It needs to be added sparingly and is usually diluted with plenty of water first to ensure it is not over used.

HP paper – watercolour paper which is hot-pressed to produce a hard, smooth surface. It is ideal for detailed work but the paint has a tendency to run very readily on it. Compare with NOT and Rough paper.

Hue – another word for colour.

Mixed media – the term used when a painting is worked in a number of different mediums. Such a painting might be worked in watercolour, gouache, coloured ink and pastel, for example.

Neutrals – colours which are hard to describe, often verging on grey or black. These are easily mixed from colours opposite each other on the colour wheel such as blue and orange. What one artist describes as neutral another artist might think is quite vibrant.

NOT paper – stands for 'not hot-pressed'. Instead the watercolour paper is cold-pressed to create a semi-rough finish. This is the most popular paper because it is the most versatile and ideal for both beginners and professionals. Compare with HP paper and Rough paper.

Oil – a painting medium made by combining pigment with oil such as linseed oil or safflower oil. Additional additives such as drier or wax may be used to improve the texture or speed the drying time, for example. Most manufacturers supply two ranges, one aimed at students and the other at professional artists. The students ranges are generally less expensive because they use cheaper pigments and sometimes contain less pigment. It is perfectly acceptable to use paints from both ranges in a painting, if desired.

Painting knives – literally knives used for painting. They have shaped blades, some quite long and thin, others short and wide that are

long and thin, others short and wide that are almost heart-shaped. Their cranked handles help keep hands clear of the paint surface and their pointed ends make a wide range of marks possible.

Palette knives – literally knives designed to be used with the palette. These are used to mix colour on the palette, to scrape the palette clean or to remove paint from the painting. They have straight, flexible blades which are longer than those on a painting knife and the handle has less of a crank. Their blunt ends make it easy to lift paint off the palette.

Pastel – sticks of pigment combined with chalk or clay and bound with gum. Soft pastels are the most widely used. Available in sticks, they contain a high proportion of pigment which means they are capable of producing really rich colour. Hard pastels contain more binder so they are firmer and create an effect more like that of a coloured pencil. Pastel pencils are pastels encased in wood and are ideal for adding detail to pastel or mixed-media work or for artists who don't like the mess of soft pastels. Oil pastels are different again. They are made by mixing pigment with animal fat and wax and combine better with oil paintings than with other pastels.

Pigment – pure dried colour which can be mixed with a binder such as gum arabic, linseed oil or egg yolk to make paint. It is available quite finely ground from art shops but it may be necessary to grind it down further before mixing it into paint.

Primary colours – red, yellow and blue. These cannot be made by mixing the other colours but in theory they can be combined to create any other colour. In practice you need a warm and cool version of each and, unless you are using watercolour, a tube of white before you can mix most hues. Even then, it is much more convenient to have a few extra colours on your palette. Compare with secondary and tertiary colours.

Rough paper – watercolour paper with a rough surface that allows the paint to settle in the hollows. This creates an attractive speckled finish. Compare with HP paper and NOT paper.

Rule of thirds – a means of creating aesthetically pleasing proportions in a composition. It involves mentally or physically dividing the support into thirds both vertically and horizontally and using these lines to arrange the composition. The points where the vertical and horizontal lines intersect are considered key positions.

Secondary colours – orange, green and violet. These are made by mixing equal quantities of two primary colours. Compare with primary and tertiary colours.

Sgraffito – the method of scratching away paint with a sharp tool to create texture.

Split complementaries – not quite complementaries. The true complementary of blue is orange, so a warm yellow would be its split complementary.

Staining – a paint which stains the paper it is applied to so that it can't be removed or which seeps into overlaid colours.

Support – the paper, canvas, panel or board on which the painting is made.

Tertiary colours – these include blue-green, red-orange and pink-violet. They are made by mixing equal quantities of a primary with the adjacent secondary. You can continue this process to mix a tertiary with a secondary and so on to create a subtle range of colours. See also primary and secondary colours.

Thinner – the substance used to dilute paint. For oils this traditionally means turpentine while for watercolour and acrylic the thinner is water.

Tone – the lightness or darkness of a colour as if the subject is seen as a black-and-white image.

Tonking – a method of removing excess oil paint from a picture to speed up drying named after its inventor, Sir Henry Tonks. It simply involves pressing a piece of absorbent paper over the wet paint and then peeling it off to remove some of the paint. The paper should not have any printed or hand-written text on it otherwise the ink may dirty the paint.

Underpainting – one of the first stages of a traditional oil painting when the elements of the composition have been painted in monochrome or very soft, bland colours. The tonal values are defined at this stage. Some artists refer to this as 'laying in'.

Watercolour – a painting medium made by combining pigment with gum arabic. A little glycerine helps to prevent the paint cracking. The quality of the paint depends mainly on the quality of the pigments used, so it's always advisable to choose a reputable brand.

Wet-in-wet – a term used to describe the watercolour technique of applying paint to wet paper or paint so the colour(s) flow and combine. It is very difficult to predict exactly what will happen with this technique but it can produce some wonderful results.

Wet-on-dry – the opposite of wet-in-wet, this simply means applying watercolour to dry paper or paint. The colour dries to form a hard edge which is useful for defining, say, the trunk of a tree.

Reading List

For information about paint colours and colour mixing you can't do better than the books by Michael Wilcox published by the School of Colour Publishing. These include 'The Artist's Guide to Selecting Colours' (ISBN 0958789185) and 'Blue and Yellow Don't Make Green' (ISBN 0958789193).

For information on specific techniques try the encyclopedia range of art books published by Headline. These include 'The Encyclopedia of Watercolour Techniques' (ISBN 0747279497); 'The Encyclopedia of Acrylic Techniques' (ISBN 0747210683); and 'The Encyclopedia of Pastel Techniques' (ISBN 0747278431).

Beginners interested in step-by-step techniques may like to refer to the painting series by Patricia Monahan and Jenny Rodwell published by Studio Vista. These include 'Oil Painting' by Patricia Monahan (ISBN 0289800587) and 'Painting in Pastels' by Jenny Rodwell (ISBN 0289800730).

Acknowledgments

Many thanks to James Ley at Winsor & Newton for supporting this book and generously supplying all the materials shown on its pages. My thanks also go to Julien Busselle for his photography, to Zoe Spencer for her picture research and to Brenda Dermody for her fabulous book design. This book would not have been possible without the inspiration and hard work of Angie Patchell at RotoVision and without the wonderful images and input of all the artists.